Teaching Social Issues in the Middle Grades

Teaching Social Issues in the Middle Grades

A Teacher's Guide to Using Case Studies to Promote Intelligent Inquiry

Selma Wassermann

ROWMAN & LITTLEFIELD
Lanham • Boulder • New York • London

Published by Rowman & Littlefield
An imprint of The Rowman & Littlefield Publishing Group, Inc.
4501 Forbes Boulevard, Suite 200, Lanham, Maryland 20706
www.rowman.com

6 Tinworth Street, London, SE11 5AL, United Kingdom

Copyright © 2021 by Selma Wassermann

All rights reserved. No part of this book may be reproduced in any form or by any electronic or mechanical means, including information storage and retrieval systems, without written permission from the publisher, except by a reviewer who may quote passages in a review.

British Library Cataloguing in Publication Information Available

Library of Congress Cataloging-in-Publication Data
Names: Wassermann, Selma, author.
Title: Teaching social issues in the middle grades : a teacher's guide to using case studies to promote intelligent inquiry / Selma Wassermann.
Description: Lanham : Rowman & Littlefield, [2021] | Includes bibliographical references and index. | Summary: "This book provides a collection of ten cases for use in the middle grades that focus on many of the critical social issues we face today"— Provided by publisher.
Identifiers: LCCN 2021009177 (print) | LCCN 2021009178 (ebook) | ISBN 9781475861044 (Cloth : acid-free paper) | ISBN 9781475861051 (Paperback : acid-free paper) | ISBN 9781475861068 (eBook)
Subjects: LCSH: Case method—Study and teaching—United States. | Social sciences—Study and teaching (Middle school)—United States. | Social science teachers—Training of—United States.
Classification: LCC LB1029.C37 W378 2021 (print) | LCC LB1029. C37 (ebook)
| DDC 372.89—dc23
LC record available at https://lccn.loc.gov/2021009177
LC ebook record available at https://lccn.loc.gov/2021009178

This one is for Simon and Arlo, who will always be my darling boys

Contents

Preface	ix
Acknowledgments	xiii
Introduction	xv
1 What Is Case Method Teaching?	1
2 Teaching with Cases? It's Not for Every Teacher	7
3 Preparing to Teach with Cases	13
4 An Instructional Design for Teaching with Cases	19
5 The Tools of the Interactive Process	31
6 Cases Based on Critical Issues in the Social Studies	45
7 What Me? A Case Writer?	79
8 Evaluating Students in a Case Method Classroom	87
9 And Finally . . .	93
Appendix: Who Makes the News?	95
Bibliography	103
Index	105
About the Author	111

Preface

I was not always a case method teacher. In fact, if truth be told, I began my teaching career by standing in front of the classroom, telling, advising, admonishing, organizing, giving information. The students, passive recipients of what I had to say, were polite, but restless. Keeping them quiet and orderly was at the top of my list of what a teacher should do. Imparting information so that they would be prepared for next year, and so that I would not be considered ineffective and wanting in my teaching skills was the primary motivator for what I did. I taught "lessons" and the students were obliged to learn the lessons.

Yes, the students learned to read with more fluency; they advanced their word analysis skills and improved their spelling. Yes, they learned the names of the important rivers in the United States, the dates of the Civil War, the names of the generals who fought in the American Revolution. In retrospect I see these as trifling achievements. Good teaching, that is, the kind of teaching that has a lasting impact on the minds and hearts of students, demands much more.

In my years of teaching teachers, I have come to the realization that most of those going into the profession hope that their teaching will make a difference in the lives of their students. Very few are satisfied with the notion that good teaching means giving lessons that are absorbed, but not lasting. Most want to make an impact, that, like the favored breakfast that farmers say, "sticks to your ribs"—the kind of breakfast food that will hold them through a morning full of strenuous chores." A stick-to-your-ribs kind of teaching?

There is, of course, more than one method, one pedagogy, one set of strategies that can accomplish such goals and in the final analysis, teachers will choose the pedagogy that is consonant with their own perceptions and beliefs of what good teaching involves. Whatever is chosen as the preferred mode, it seems that all "stick to your ribs" teaching have similar components.

Each has its roots in methods that require students to think on higher cognitive levels than merely acquiring information. Each accommodates for an individual learner's developmental level and idiosyncratic learning style. Each demonstrates respect for every student. Each provides freedom for learners to say what they think, without condemnation. Each emphasizes "what's important"—that is, those important issues that warrant serious and thoughtful inquiry. Each allows students to take those giant steps toward becoming more wise, more informed, more intelligent, more discerning, and kinder to each other.

Observing a case teaching session will, very quickly, demonstrate that this pedagogy fulfills all of the above goals, without equivocation.

It is a pedagogy that has long been associated with the highest quality of instruction at the Harvard Business School, where cases of actual companies are dissected and analyzed by students to better understand the complex factors involved in business management. Cases are also widely used in medical ethics courses. In the New Pathway Program at the Harvard Medical School teaching with cases is the primary instructional method in the training of doctors.

The past few years have seen increased attention to teaching with cases in schools of education. Textbooks containing a wealth of in-school cases, in which aspiring teachers must wrestle with the dilemmas of classroom practice are widely available.

Where case method teaching has made the most impressive inroads is, I believe, in secondary schools. Spurred by the work of a small group of teachers at the Centennial Secondary School in British Columbia, teaching with cases has now become a viable modus operandi in virtually every school subject, including mathematics, biology, general science, English, government, history, and family life. Teachers who have adopted this approach talk about renewed enthusiasm for teaching. Students are pressing to get into their classes. The evidence is mounting that something good is going on. It is not that these classes are "easy" and undemanding; it is that they offer students a chance to be engaged at a level heretofore unseen in other classes, a chance to use their minds, to be excited about issues of consequence, to find meaning in their classroom experiences.

Can case method teaching be a viable pedagogy in the middle grades? Those teachers who have chosen to write cases that are appropriate for middle grade level students and have tried them out with their classes report not only success, but enthusiasm. Students engage eagerly; there are no shirkers. Once the guidelines for student participation are made explicit, once the students know and appreciate their roles, the demands, the processes, they seem to have little difficulty rising to the occasion.

The payoffs are sweet.

Rich Chambers taught his first case, "A Case of Injustice in Our Time" about the internment of Japanese-American citizens during WWII—the beginning of his social studies class's investigations of racial prejudice. The students had read the case as a homework assignment and, back in class, entered into small discussion groups to deal with the questions appending the case. The group discussions were heated and active; the teacher went from group to group, listening, but not intervening.

Directly after the group discussions, Rich called the class together for "debriefing"—a whole class discussion centering on the important issues of the case. Using his finely honed interactive skills in conducting the discussion, Rich's questions probed at the heart of the issues. A flurry of students' hands shot up, each vying for "air time."

One boy offered that the Japanese got what they deserved since they had bombed Pearl Harbor. At this, many students wanted to offer contrary views, and it was clear that there was divided opinion on the issue. Close to the end of class, one student, Yoshimi, of Japanese descent, offered quite mournfully: "I am getting the notion, from listening to some of you that if that was happening to me and my family, none of you would stand up for us."

The class went silent. She had brought the issues in the case "home"; this could be happening to her and her family. This was not just a school exercise. This was real.

The bell rang and the students grudgingly filed out into the hall, each still talking about the case. As Rich watched them he said, "Now that's what I call social studies."

For those students, that case had a memorable "stick to your ribs" effect. Contacts with a few of them years later gave evidence that that particular case had deep significance for them in their growing understanding and appreciation of the insidious and harmful acts of racism. Some of them became engaged in antiracist organizations, where they could play an active role in support of their beliefs. Many remembered the impact of the case on their thinking. Many remarked on the power of learning with cases.

In my years of teaching, I have come to the belief that not all teachers are cut out for teaching with cases. Some are hard wired into beliefs that teaching "lessons" is what matters and what they prefer to do. And no amount of contrary data will convince them otherwise.

On the other hand, some teachers have become dissatisfied with what they are doing, dissatisfied with the results on student behavior, dissatisfied with their perception of what teaching can be. As Laura B. put it: "My classes were boring and I came to the realization that it was me that was boring."

But having embraced teaching with cases, she never looked back. The clear evidence of what happens to students and the pure joy of teaching a case well—that kind of exhilaration is hard to find in teaching lessons.

For those teachers who are looking for that kind of teaching experience—teaching that has that stick-to-the-ribs quality and that offers the promise of elevating students' thinking about important issues, the materials in this book are offered with my own very good wishes to each for the kind of teaching that fulfills your most gratifying expectations.

Acknowledgments

There are many to whom I am indebted for helping me to see this book to completion and I would like to offer them all my deepest and most sincere thanks, acknowledging their help, advice, and encouragement in this process that all writers know to be a challenge.

Simon Snow, the wizard of Parksville, is always at the ready with his help and support with all things technical. Without Simon, I'd still be writing in pencil on a yellow pad. Maya, the adorable, gives me up-to-date information about middle graders and their competence to address specific challenges. Kai teaches me patience and introduces me to the wonders of what tablets can do. My good friend and colleague, Larry Cuban field tested several cases with his granddaughter, Barbaraciela and gave me feedback that informed further editing on the cases. Arlo and Ruben keep me sane. Paula is my one-woman support system. Colleague Tom O'Shea gave his permission to use an excerpt from our jointly written case, "The Yahagi Maru." Paul Odermatt, likewise, gave permission to use material from his case, "Who Makes the News?"

Teachers College Press, of Columbia University granted permission for me to adapt material from my previously published books with them. These permissions have been cited in the text. And finally, to Tom Koerner and the editorial staff at Rowman & Littlefield, my heartfelt thanks for your confidence in my work and for helping to see this book to its final stage.

Introduction

Before considering a methodology that advocates the use of cases to elevate students' understanding and analysis of relevant social issues, teachers will want to ask themselves at least three questions:

- Is case method teaching an appropriate pedagogy for middle grades?
- Is case method teaching an appropriate pedagogy for teaching social issues?
- How were the social issues in this book selected?

This chapter will begin to address these questions as well as provide evidence to support the work of this book.

CASE METHOD TEACHING IN THE MIDDLE GRADES

It is true that the roots of case method teaching are found in the Graduate School of Business at Harvard University. From there, its reputation as an effective way of elevating students' intelligent habits of thinking about important issues spread—at first, to other professional schools at Harvard, and then to other business and professional schools in the United States, Canada, and abroad (Wassermann, 1994).

Beginning in 1990, the pedagogy began to filter down into secondary schools in British Columbia (Wassermann, 1994). The success of these initial experiences led to increased attention and more widespread use of cases in secondary schools throughout Canada, the United States, and in Sweden. In each situation, where cases were tried and used in classes across several curriculum areas, the student response was sufficiently gratifying to ensure that once initiated, cases as pedagogical tools took firm hold.

Courses offered at Simon Fraser University as electives for teachers interested in writing their own cases and in applying the methodology in their own classrooms were oversubscribed; there seemed to be a surge of interest and attention in case method teaching, spread, no doubt by teachers' and students' enthusiasm and clear signs of its effectiveness.

More than a few textbooks appeared (Kleinfeld, 1989; Christensen, Garvin and Sweet, 1991; Shulman, 1992; Silverman and Welty, 1992; Wheatley, 1986) that offered additional insights into the pedagogy as well as observations on its use in different subject areas. Without exception, each of these volumes showed the application of case method teaching to the higher education levels. It wasn't until 1990 that case method teaching began to filter down into the secondary school—first in a trickle, and then in a flood (Wassermann, 1992; 1994).

For social studies teachers, the ways in which the method incorporated social problems drawn from real events in the curriculum had enormous appeal—especially when such positive results were seen in students' responses and in their enthusiasm for those classes. Teachers were more than persuaded of Dewey's critique (1938) that "education is not an affair of telling and being told, but an active and constructive process, not a pouring in, not learning by passive absorption."

The first recorded example of a case used in the elementary school occurred when a third-grade teacher (Hood, 1992) used a case she had written with her students. The case reflected an incident that occurred in her classroom, when an important "trophy" that a boy had brought to school, and lent to a friend, went missing. The case centered on issues of responsibility, friendship, trust, and protecting one's possessions. Spurred on by the immediate and positive success of the students' engagement and their obvious willingness to dig into the critical issues led to Hood's writing of other cases, and their subsequent use with her class.

Hood's cases (as well as dozens of others written by teachers) are available online, at the Simon Fraser University Case Clearing House. They are offered without charge and may be downloaded and duplicated for classroom use (http://www.sfu.ca/education/centres-offices/ec/resources/.html).

To answer the first question: is case method teaching an appropriate pedagogy for middle grade students—the answer, based on many elementary school teachers' experiences is an unequivocal yes.

USING CASES TO TEACH SOCIAL ISSUES

Teaching social issues is not new to middle grade curriculum. Even a cursory glance at the curriculum standards for most states will reveal that historical, civic, economic, and geographic issues are at front and center of what is included for study. For example, the Grade 5 curriculum for California states that "students will continue to develop the civic and economic skills they will need as citizens, especially as they learn about the nation's foundational documents ... instruction that is framed around questions of historic significance" (California Department of Education, 2017).

In worst case scenarios however, social issues are taught as "givens" – situations that have occurred in history and have been "resolved." Yes, the Native Americans were displaced by the government of the United States to make room for the settlers, farmers, and ranchers. Yes, slaves were transported from Africa to the southern states to be bought and sold as property, and that was bad. Yes, the Civil War was fought to free the slaves. Yes, the earliest civilizations in China produced many innovations that are still widely used. Yes, major imperial governments in Europe sent men and ships to colonize lands in America, Africa, and Asia and brought germs that decimated native populations. Yes, women gained the right to vote in the United States in 1920. To "know" these facts is to know hardly anything about these issues.

In truth, social issues, like most real life issues, are full of complexities and conundrums, laden with questions that are still unresolved. In many cases, social issues have no "happy ending." Even when they have become accepted "facts of history," they are still subject to uncertainties. For example, when women gained the right to vote in 1920, how did that bring more equality between the sexes? When Lincoln signed the Emancipation Proclamation, how did the United States make reparations to the slaves for their imprisonment and their labors? What were some of the more egregious failures of Reconstruction? What was the result of the westward movement on the lives of the Native Americans displaced from their lands? How did the colonization of African states impact their later development?

Yes, social issues are messy, and defy clear, unambiguous answers. This is why using cases to teach social issues makes the most sense—because cases, in themselves, raise the kinds of ambiguities that are embedded in social issues. They give students a chance to wrestle with these ambiguities, from cognitive and affective vantage points, to learn to suspend judgment, to reason from the data however insufficient, to use hard evidence to support their ideas. Cases take students into the heart of the issues—and allow them to get inside the reality of what has occurred. Perhaps one of the most important outcomes is for students to learn to live with uncertainty. That is not a small goal.

In fact, there may be no better pedagogy to teach social issues than using case studies.

SELECTING THE SOCIAL ISSUES

If one scans the curriculum guides for middle schools, it is possible to find dozens of issues that would serve as a basis for creating case studies. So selecting social issues to create cases was not difficult. What was difficult was sorting through the many possibilities and choosing the ones that seemed most relevant, must current, most appropriate for serious student consideration at the time of this writing. Yes, it is true that contemporary situations, examined from an historical perspective weighed heavily on the decision of what to include.

Doubtless, teachers across the land will take issue with some of what has been included and what has been omitted. In the first instance, the writer pleads bias; and will affirm that these are the issues that seemed most critical for students' serious consideration. In the second instance, issues that have been omitted may be addressed by teachers writing their own cases, to include issues that have been overlooked. Some suggestions for writing cases have been included in later chapters, but the cases themselves should serve as guides for a teacher's creative efforts in case writing.

At the time of this writing, the world has been seized by a pandemic that has resulted in over 200,000 deaths in the United States alone. A vast majority of Americans have been huddled at home, in quarantine, fearful, anxious, and in a strange kind of limbo. The shutting of businesses has led to mass unemployment, hunger, homelessness. Schools have opened, and then closed. Travel is restricted and some countries have closed their borders. Wearing a face mask is now de rigueur—although more than a few people have insisted on their "civil right" to ignore the best medical advice, refusing to wear them, putting themselves and others recklessly at risk. Is this a social issue that should be studied? How can it be ignored?

The current news is full of the president's claims of potential fraud in the election. The President's tweet that "Rigged 2020 election millions of mail-in ballots will be printed by foreign countries, and others. It will be the scandal of our times!" (Rutenberg, 2020). What will happen now that President Trump has been defeated and he has refused to concede? Is this a social issue that warrants students' serious study? How can it be ignored?

So yes, personal bias of what this writer sees as important for middle grade students to study went to the top of the list of criteria for selection. Curriculum guides also played a key role in those selections. These are offered not only as examples of what can be taught in raising students' awareness of important social issues and their various dimensions and implications, but also providing them with the experiences of delving deeply into these issues, with heart and mind, to make "meaning" of the what, how, and why of these complex situations.

IN RETROSPECT

In this writer's view, learning that has no emotional component is sterile. It withers and dries and fades away quickly. Perhaps that is why students "lose" more than 85% of what they had "learned" between June and September.

Learning that has an emotional component has resonance; it lingers and remains, as it continues to churn and spin in the mind, sifting and sorting in a meaning-making vortex. In the hands of a skilled teacher, teaching with cases can make a significant difference in the quality of students' learning about social issues. It is for teachers to decide if this is what they truly want.

"Remember that case we studied last year? I'm still thinking about it."

Chapter 1

What Is Case Method Teaching?

SCENES FROM THE CLASSROOM

Paul O. was teaching the case "Who Makes the News?" (Odermatt, 1991; see appendix) to his Grade 7 students. The case is concerned with the ways in which events are manipulated by the media, to elevate what makes for more viewer interest, rather than what is accurate. The case is centered on questions of media responsibility, the dividing line between news reporting and entertainment, and what, of what is seen on TV and read on the Internet can be believed to be an accurate representation of "truth."

The students began work by reading the case as a homework assignment. At the beginning of the class session the students gathered in small groups to discuss the case questions:

1. *In your view, what parts of the scenes presented about students would be most accurate? What data from the case support your view of accuracy?*
2. *In your view, what parts of the program presented about students would be the least accurate? What data from the case support your view?*
3. *In this case, certain factors influenced Lori and Jenny's behavior. How do you explain it? How is a person's behavior influenced by certain conditions in an immediate situation?*
4. *As you see it, what role did Martin and Bill play in "shaping" the afternoon session?*
5. *The video that was being filmed in this case was scheduled to be shown during "ratings week." How, in your opinion, might this have contributed to the shaping of this show?*

Following the study group discussions, the teacher called the class together to debrief the case. Paul's debriefing centered on the "big ideas" that the case put under examination. This is a brief example of that discussion.

Paul: I'd like to begin by asking you to tell me what you think about the ways in which media reports accurately represent the news they are supposed to cover.

At first, the students are silent; Paul waits.

Heather: Well, it's clear to me that in the case, the way in which the TV crew manipulated the situation, so that they could present a particular point of view was disgusting. I mean, how could we believe what we saw in the program knowing how that situation was manufactured.

Paul: The case gives you some evidence that the filming situation was, as you say, "manufactured?"

Heather: Yeh. They set it up to show what they wanted to show.

Paul: So what came out, as a result, I mean, the actual showing of the program, was not an accurate portrayal of these girls?

Heather: Yes, that's right. It made me angry.

Paul: Thanks for your thoughts, Heather. I want to ask others to weigh in here.

Yusef: I agree with Heather. They started by having the girls dress up, putting on mascara and eye shadow and make-up to make them look older. I think they wanted them to look more sexy. And they are only 12. I mean, give me a break.

Paul: You too sound a bit mad at what the TV crew did to change the look of the girls who were being interviewed. So in the way they got the girls to put make up on, that was not an accurate representation of what they actually looked like.

Yusef: Yeh. It was, as Heather said, manufactured. They are shaping the events so that we would come to a conclusion they wanted for us.

Paul: They had an agenda in mind and they constructed the situation so that we would come to the conclusion they wanted for us?

Yusef: Yes. It was completely untrustworthy.

Paul: So what did this tell us about accuracy in reporting?

In this brief scenario, the key elements of case teaching are revealed. At first, the teacher chooses the case that represents the social issue he wants students to study. The students prepare the case by reading it in advance of class and thinking about the questions appended to the case. When they return to class, they engage in small study groups to discuss the questions. This is followed by the teachers' subsequent debriefing—a whole class discussion that centers on the big ideas of the case—those important issues that the teacher believes essential to examine.

During debriefing, the teacher's interactions are never judgmental. They don't explain or give information. Instead, skillful questioning and responding skills allow the teacher to work with students' ideas, helping them to examine assumptions, calling for data to support ideas, elevating inconsistencies in thinking, and differences in points of view. All of this is done respectfully, without judgment in word or tone, and the climate is safe for any student to venture an opinion. An important goal in debriefing is that students learn to reason from the data and to assume responsibility for their ideas.

In this way students learn to think more intelligently about the issues and understanding grows. Students are more willing to volunteer their ideas and the amount of class participation is often close to 100%. No one notices that the class time is up; no one wants to leave. Both cognitive and affective dimensions of learning are clearly evident.

WHAT ARE CASES?

Cases are complex educational instruments that are constructed around pivotal, real life issues that appear in the form of narratives. Their content includes information and hard data, psychological and anthropological observations, and technical material. They are drawn from specific curriculum areas, such as history, economics, government, bioethics, medical ethics but the narrative threads are interdisciplinary in nature.

Each case is rooted in certain "big ideas"—those significant issues that call for serious and in-depth study. Because cases are written as real life problems confronting humans, their narratives are compelling and immediately engage students' interest (Coles, 1990).

Some students commenting on their work in case method classrooms have written:

This is my most enjoyable class and I learn the most of out this class than any other class. I think the social issues and your cases are great!
Your class is more interesting and I pay more attention.
Best class and most enjoyable that I've ever had. Learning can be exciting and fun. This class proves it. I'm learning a lot more and my grades can verify it.
This is probably the most interesting and fun class. Our group discussions help me learn more because I get involved.
I don't think I've ever enjoyed social studies as much as I do this year. I always look forward to this class and I really enjoy the assignments (Adam, 1991).

Lawrence (1953) has written, "A good case is the vehicle by which a chunk of reality is brought into the classroom to be worked over by the class and the instructor. It keeps the class discussion grounded upon some of the stubborn facts that must be faced in real life situations. It is the anchor on academic flights of speculation. It is the record of complex situations that must be literally pulled apart and put together again for the expression of attitudes or ways of thinking brought into the classroom."

WHAT DOES TEACHING BY THE CASE METHOD LOOK LIKE?

Case method teaching offers a clear alternative to traditional instruction in nearly every way. More traditional approaches rely primarily on the dissemination of information to students who, generally, sit quietly to absorb the information. Teachers who use this approach will lecture, give examples, draw on information from primary sources, present graphs and charts, show films and videos. In this more traditional approach, it is the teacher who is always in control of the action.

In teaching with cases, the teacher develops or locates cases that contain within them the big ideas, or major concepts to be studied. The students read the case as a homework assignment, and then, upon returning to class, work in small groups to discuss the study questions that accompany the case. Students are held responsible for expanding their knowledge base in their examination of the issues and concepts, lest their discussions lead to distorted and immature conclusions. Information is gathered not from the teacher's lectures but from the reading and gathering of documentary material.

This initial study and small group discussions form the basis for the teacher's follow-up work with the students: debriefing the case. Debriefing calls for the kind of discussion in which teachers' questions and responses, carefully formulated, require students to reach for deeper meanings from within the content, and to use data in support of their ideas. The teacher's role shifts from disseminating information to extracting meanings. Because no single correct answers are sought, and because complex issues have many sides, debriefing creates a tension that drives highly motivated subsequent inquiries.

This allows the teacher to supplement the case with additional resources as follow up: texts, journal articles, newspaper articles, novels, films, photo essays, and other sources that are woven into subsequent class lessons. Issues are examined through multifaceted, interdisciplinary lenses and are viewed from real life conditions in which they actually arise. When a case has power—that is, when it is written in a compelling narrative form, and when the teacher is skillful in debriefing, these conditions stimulate students' interests and motivate them to know more. It sets the scene for further study. As some students put it:

Case study method has had a dramatic effect on how I learn because if you don't understand something you feel free to ask. Everyone has a chance to voice their ideas and I believe this form of learning helps to bring the class together.

When coming to this class I had no idea of some of the problems in the world today. Race, religion, etc. Now after five months, I feel as if I know a lot more. I can now sit in class and look at two different points of view, rather than just seeing my own. Not only have I noticed my change, but family and friends have too.

The case study method allows you to listen to other points of view, consider them and then form an analysis of the issue using these other points of view. A better understanding of the issue is possible.

Case study method has broadened my way of thinking on certain issues.

When you share ideas with the whole class you get a lot of new ideas and a better understanding of the topic.

I have learned how to listen to other people and to understand that there are many different interpretations of one topic.

No memorization involved which takes the pressure off and you think clearer.

It opened new doors for me to understand the issues.

A textbook has no feelings, but all sorts of feelings come out in the groups.

From the textbook you can only get facts. But I found that with case studies you found out how others feel about certain issues and from these beliefs you can make a judgment (Adam, 1991).

END NOTES

Many teachers already know that if you want the "skinny"—that is, if you really and truly want to know about the effectiveness of what you are doing, you need to ask the students. But you need to ask them in a way that protects them from any possible repercussions that might come from speaking their opinions honestly. In virtually every case method class, anonymous comments from students are very similar to the above. Case method teaching classes have a vitality and a sense of purpose that is palpable. Not only do students enjoy these classes, but the evidence is great that they benefit in numerous ways—that is, in the very many ways that are highlighted in course outlines with goals emphasizing the promotion of critical thinking.

Case method teaching delivers on its promise to promote the intelligent examination of important issues.

Chapter 2

Teaching with Cases? It's Not for Every Teacher

SCENES FROM THE TEACHERS' WORKSHOP

Twenty-six social studies teachers arrived to participate in a district-sponsored series of professional-day workshops to develop teachers' skills in using case method teaching. It was understood, at the outset, that participation was strictly voluntary. The teacher group consisted largely of veteran teachers, most of whom had "been around the block," and had earned their "creds" as experienced teachers.

At the second session, the number present was down to sixteen. At the third, only six teachers showed up. Before checking out, one teacher confronted the workshop leader, saying that he was unable to embrace the concept of case method teaching because, to him, "cases had too much impact." He was worried about the influence that cases might have on his students.

He went further to claim that he believed it was dangerous to use material that went beyond the facts. "The textbook," he said, "was neutral. There are no biases in textbook material. Students just get the plain facts. I see teaching history as teaching students certifiable truths. I just don't see how cases would fit into the way my courses are taught."

The workshop leader responded: "I see what you mean. Given what you have told me, I too cannot see how teaching with cases would fit in with your teaching goals. I have a suspicion that teaching with cases would be very unsettling for you."

Relinquishing Control

From all that has been written so far about case method teaching, it is clear that this pedagogy involves giving more control over to the students—control in the sense that they have considerably more agency over the learning process. The teacher does facilitate the discussion but does not take part in the study groups. This "facilitation" does not involve telling or instructing or advocating. It has an entirely different shape, one that puts the onus of thinking into the students' domain.

Of course, a teacher's skill in debriefing is essential to produce the kind of thoughtful inquiry into the issues, shifting student thinking away from opinions that are highly prejudiced, assumptions that go far beyond the data, and ideas that seem to come from left field. And in this sense, the teacher does have control over that process; but in the overall, it is the students who are the ones who are actively and productively engaged.

The giving over of control to students is not easy for some teachers for it requires what might be considered an abandonment of responsibility to oversee every action, every move, every part of every process of teaching. This is the way in which some teachers conceive of what teaching is.

Yet, others believe that one important goal of teaching is to promote the learner's independence, to create a climate in the classroom that motivates students to take their own steps, to develop ownership of the how and the what of their studies. For teachers with these beliefs, teaching with cases will be easily embraced. For those who have difficulty relinquishing control, teaching with cases may be anathema.

Teachers' beliefs, whether consciously chosen or unconsciously held, lie at the heart of most classroom decisions and hence actions. What a teacher believes is what a teacher does. A pedagogy that is not congruent with a teacher's beliefs is not likely to be chosen and if imposed, is not likely to endure. For teachers to feel satisfied, they will use a methodology that is congruent with their deepest beliefs about teaching, about learning, about their students. All of us need to find satisfaction in our work.[1]

Teachers, of course, have other needs and these are more personal and often unconscious. Unlike beliefs that are chosen, we do not choose our needs. Rather they choose us. What then is to be made of the connection between personal needs, like "control needs" and the potential risks involved in putting into operation an innovative methodology like case method teaching? Only this: that before a teacher embarks on a plan that may be radically different from past experience, it might be worthwhile to make some personal, private assessment, to consider how one's own psychological needs may facilitate or stand in the way of effective implementation.

This kind of self-scrutiny is not for the more timid; but it is a route to determine whether you see yourself as a potential case method teacher or would rather prefer and feel safer in an altogether different classroom ethos. If you are considering case method teaching, consider what you are likely to gain and what you are likely to lose in deciding for or against teaching with cases.

A Teacher Decides

The need for success in teaching is present in all teachers. We want to see our students moving forward in what and how they are learning. We want to see our important educational goals realized in their behaviors. No teacher will be content with evidence that his or her goals have been subverted, or that students are far from responsive participants.

To help to allay some of teachers' concerns before choosing case method teaching, it may be helpful to provide a few concrete suggestions about procedures that might ease the way into successful classroom applications.

How Will I Give Grades?

In some classrooms, grades are major determinants in what teachers and students do. "Will this be on the test?" is the litmus test of what students believe is important to learn, to know, to remember. If it's not going to be graded, then why bother to learn it?

When case method teaching is the method du jour, grades seem to take a back seat to what else is going on. Engagement in the process, in the study groups and in the debriefing, the serious consideration of the important issues seem to rise above other concerns. Not all students will be disabused of the notion that grades are secondary to what is learned; but perhaps there are ways to satisfy both goals.

A radical approach is to allow students the chance to evaluate themselves. Oh yes, this has been tried and proven successful in many classes that have chosen case method teaching. It would start with the teacher's design of an evaluative instrument that would highlight what that teacher considered important criteria, such as:

How would you evaluate your work in the study groups?
How would you assess your participation in the debriefing discussions?
How would you assess your contributions to the discussions?
What evidence can you provide to show what you have learned?

Questions such as these would give students additional control over the process, and their responses would give teachers data from which to make determinations about a grade.

Of course, not all subjects in the class would be offered via case method. So there would be other forms of data upon which teachers might make fair and thoughtful judgments about students' performance. Case method teaching does not impede the careful and thoughtful consideration of students' grades. (More about evaluating students is found in chapter 8.)

How Will I Cover the Curriculum?

It will be seen that not all the cases included in this text address all curriculum issues for all grade levels in different school districts. Some will; some may, with a stretch. Teachers can choose from the cases included here those that most closely relate to learning standards for the grade.

The cases included address a selected group of social issues that may stretch beyond the grade standards, yet be, in the teacher's judgment, of value to study. Once again, choosing what seems more appropriate and more relevant is part of the teacher's job.

And of course, not every social studies lesson will be taught with cases. So there are more degrees of freedom for teachers, even those who use a large sample of case teaching methods.

Won't It Be Too Noisy?

Of course there will be a distinct hum of voices in the study groups. This is expected; but why should that be a problem? It is generally the case that students listen respectfully and quietly during the debriefing. If that is not the case, then something amiss is going on.

Can I Trust the Students to Work Responsibly?

In most situations, when teachers have behavioral standards for class activities, they make these explicit. For example, when teachers take students on a field trip, standards of behavior are provided beforehand—so students know what is expected. When introducing case method teaching to a class, standards should also be explicit and clear.

These behavioral standards for students would include, first, a priori preparation—that is, the careful reading of the case before class. In other words, being prepared. Second, it would include standards for work in the study groups. A few teachers have made charts that are posted in the classroom that advise and recommend study group participation. For example, respectful listening and attending to the statements of others; waiting one's turn to speak; never responding with hurtful or derogatory comments; giving all a chance to participate. Since most teachers understand the need to orient students to new experiences, this is probably a no-brainer. More about study groups, and their preparation is found in a later chapter.

Will Parents Accept This Approach?

In this writer's experience, there is no single methodology that will please all parents all the time. But it is the case that most, if not all, parents want the best for the children. And evidence that children are learning and enthusiastic about school is the one huge "tell" that will allay parental concerns.

It may be helpful that teachers embarking on case method teaching bring the parents "on side"—that is, give them some advance organizers about why these cases are being used, what are the important advantages, and what are some learning outcomes to be expected. It is doubtful that any parent will oppose the development of students' intelligent habits of thinking that is one key goal of teaching with cases.

END NOTES

Returning to the comments of the teacher described in the opening paragraph, it is clear that using case method teaching is not compatible with every teacher's beliefs of what constitutes the teaching/learning process. When teachers believe that students are unable to assume responsibility for their learning; that cases take too much time; that curriculum must be covered sequentially; that the teacher's role is that of disseminator of information; that cases will not allow students to pass the standardized tests; that students will not work responsibly in groups; that learning means knowing all the right answers; that teachers must be in control of the action at all times—it is doubtful that this book would prove otherwise to them.

But there is a large group of teachers who see these methods and strategies compatible with their hopes, dreams, and beliefs for what and how their students should be learning, about what's important in teaching, about how best to facilitate students' understandings of the big ideas in the social studies. For these teachers, the chapters that follow include the key "ingredients" of case teaching methodology. These should provide teachers with the tools to navigate the what, why, and how of putting these methods to work in middle grade classrooms.

If previous experiences of many case method teachers have any relevance, the results seen in what students can do will more than assure teachers that case method teaching can and does fulfill the most important educational goals of the middle grades.

NOTE

1. Adapted by permission of the Publisher. From Selma Wassermann, *Introduction to Case Method Teaching: A Guide to the Galaxy*. New York: Teachers College Press. Copyright © 1994 by Teachers College, Columbia University. All rights reserved.

Chapter 3

Preparing to Teach with Cases

SCENES FROM THE CLASSROOM

Student: If the topic is controversial I find myself debating with other students in the class and the rest of the day and sometimes the next day. Case studies may change people our age to be more concerned with what is happening around them.

Understanding the Teaching Framework

Teaching with cases uses an instructional design in which the threads of teaching for thinking, active learning, students working in groups, and power theory combine to form the instructional matrix of the curriculum experience (Wassermann, 1990). The design incorporates the following components:

1. Students' active engagement on the learning task. In their reading of the cases and their discussion of case study questions, students work in cooperative learning groups to carry out discussions of the big ideas on which the case is centered. Because the study questions are framed to promote higher-order thinking, the cognitive demands are greater than the demands of searching for "right answers." The students are "on their own" in the study groups; consequently, they have greater control over their own learning, and this control increases their sense of personal power.
2. Debriefing. During debriefing, teachers use certain instructional strategies (teacher-student interactions) that probe for deeper meaning of the big ideas. Debriefing promotes students' thoughtful reflection on the issues.
3. Follow-up activities. Students' high motivation and increased interest drive their further inquiries. Issues are re-examined from a variety of perspectives in supplementary texts, novels, films, journal articles, newspaper reports, and other related source material. As a result, students gain more knowledge as well as deeper understanding.

The instructional design is cyclical and evolves in more complex spirals of inquiry in which ideas and issues undergo intensive, repeated scrutiny from different and new perspectives. Student thinking is constantly challenged.

In the Beginning

What is presented here is a brief overview of what teachers may do to inform and prepare themselves as case teachers. More complete information, including examples, guidelines, and teaching strategies is provided in later chapters.

1. Begin by studying the case and the case study questions. This means being intimately acquainted with the material in the case, the key issues, the "big ideas" underlying the case, and being knowledgeable about the background material that supports the case. That may require reading information from the social studies textbook, from related articles in current events, from historic documents, from other relevant sources of accurate and reliable information.
2. Becoming familiar with debriefing skills. This is the harsh reality: debriefing skills are not learned in a day. They are not learned from reading about them in a text or from listening to lectures. They are learned from the teacher's ability to perceive the differences in the interactive dialogue between questions and responses that call for examination of ideas and those that call for answers and equally important, from the teacher's increasing awareness of him/herself in the act of debriefing.

Learning to listen to self, and to perceive what is coming out of one's mouth, as well as observing the impact of those statements and questions on student responses is, not to put it too bluntly, the sine qua non of improving one's debriefing skills.

What follows from this initial perception is the teacher's commitment and inclination to initiate this kind of interactive dialogue with students, being constantly alert to his or her own questioning and responding techniques and working consistently to make the modifications that result in increased competence with debriefing skills.

In learning the art of debriefing teachers are advised to begin an in-classroom program of practice with an emphasis on self-scrutiny. For those intrepid teachers who wish to master these skills, a helpful medium for learning to listen to self is a recorder or video camera.

There is, alas, no shortcut to mastery. But no mistake: skillful debriefing is one of the critical strategies to successful case method teaching.

Some comments from students who have been at the other end of debriefing have this to say:

There were no right or wrong answers. I could talk and explain myself without keeping it in.

I am more willing to speak out.

I feel I can communicate more. When I first came into class I was very shy and did not want to say anything because I was afraid of what the others would think of me. But now, if I have something to say I can. I know that I will not be judged because of it.

I am becoming more comfortable expressing my ideas out loud to the class.

I have never been a talkative person in class until I came to this class. Now I speak freely and express my thoughts and feelings about issues.

The case study process gives the students an atmosphere and surrounding where they feel comfortable. This increased my ability to communicate and understand other people's points of view which is critical out in the real world.

You feel a little nervous to speak at first. No one wanted to be the first speaker, but once the discussion started, the class really gets into the work. By the middle of the semester people felt very comfortable sitting down and talking about issues. This also helped some people communicate out of class. They learn how to explain themselves.

I think that if all my classes were taught in this method, I would have a very high mark. This method makes learning less boring. This way I have discussed it, expressed my opinion, and heard others. I have learned, not memorized.

This method had me hooked from day one. You learn much more information than a text could provide, and it is a lot more exciting.

I have learned that everyone's point of view is valid and must be respected.

Everyone respects each other's answers or feelings. No one laughs but you do get a good debate out of some of the people. I love it.

In ten years from now, many won't remember what they read from a textbook, but they will remember a lot more about what we did with case studies (Adam, 1991).

Implications of Case Method Teaching

As every choice is followed by consequences, so does the choice of case method teaching have important implications for teachers, students, and for the life of the classroom. If teachers shift their teaching actions from more traditional methods to cases, what might be some of those consequences?

Students. From the student comments above, it is clear that students are more actively involved when cases are being used. Students show more responsibility in working together without teacher supervision. There is a virtual absence of the need to "manage behavior." At the outer edge of this is students' willingness to express openly feelings and ideas that may reveal negative attitudes or ideas that teachers find repugnant.

While this may be hard to live with, the top side is the teacher's opportunity to discover that some students believe these things. This provides them with the opportunity to help these students to re-evaluate such ideas. In other methods of teaching, such ideas might never see the light of day.

The data from student surveys also reveal more interest in the issues, more willingness to express opinions, more discussion and reading out of class. Because students are more interested, they are generally more prepared. In classes where cases are being used, students say they enjoy the classes more and they suggest that this enjoyment and learning has a relationship to improved grades.

Teachers. Teachers suggest that teaching with cases is never boring! The amount of student interest, participation, and involvement is exciting and motivating for teachers.

There is no doubt that teaching with cases means giving control over learning to the students. A teacher has to feel quite secure to do that and quite committed to this approach to allow that control to pass from teacher to students. A teacher must be committed to the notion that students do learn important information from work with cases and must be able to relinquish his or her role as information disseminator as well as a constant judge of students' statements.

A teacher must be comfortable with nonsequential learning, appreciating that students do grow to understand important issues when they study content in nonsequential ways. A teacher must be comfortable with a classroom in which the noise from small group discussion is the norm; must appreciate that the road to learning is not necessarily a silent journey. These are some of the implications for teachers who would choose teaching with cases.

Evaluation. Since evaluation procedures are the "tails that wag the dogs" of curriculum, the way the teacher chooses to evaluate student learning is the reality of "what's important" to learn in that class. If, for example, classroom tests continue to emphasize memorization and recall of information, then case study teaching will not "fly" in that classroom. The students will know, implicitly and explicitly, that issues and understandings are not important. What's important are names, dates, and places. In other words, such classroom tests will virtually cancel out any benefits of teaching with cases.

Classroom evaluation that is consistent with case method teaching must be rooted in the examination of issues. That means tests that use the kind of higher-order questions similar to those found at the end of each of the cases. Such higher-order questions will reveal students' understanding of the issues and will assess what teachers want to find out about the depth of student understanding.

While this may put an increased burden of reading students' papers on the already overburdened teacher, and while it means that teachers will have to do some problem solving to keep this burden manageable, evaluation practices must be congruent with case method teaching if the important learning outcomes are to be realized.

No classroom, whether cases are used or not, should be a hothouse where testing students' knowledge takes precedence over all other forms of learning. So even if a teacher chooses exams that ask students to write about what they think and what they have understood, using such tests less frequently should reduce the burden of marking on the teacher.

Further to the point, there are other ways to assess students' knowledge and understanding. A few teachers in the Centennial School Case Study Project Team (1991) instead of classroom tests, used "projects" in which students were asked to create two-or three-dimensional products to demonstrate some important concepts that had been learned with specific cases. Many examples of the kinds of projects that students could undertake are found in chapter 8.

END NOTES

Perhaps it is a mistake for someone advocating the benefits of teaching with cases to present, alongside of those benefits, some of the downsides for teachers to consider. But it does seem that representing "what is" in a truthful manner, rather than stirring up a storm of enthusiasm that might end in disappointment and frustration, is a more honest and effective approach.

Teachers have been led down the garden path before—with promises of potential "wins" and "gains" and "successes" that are doomed to failure because the promised method, strategy, program did not deliver, or had too many unexamined flaws to make it effective. That is why it seemed more reasonable to present, with clarity and accuracy, the upside and downside of teaching with cases.

Some teachers reading the above may be put off; that would be sad. But for those who have found these introductory chapters alluring, beckoning, inviting, and consonant with what they want for their students, the chapters that follow will offer more specific help as well as classroom materials to set you on the pathway to become a case method teacher.

Chapter 4

An Instructional Design for Teaching with Cases

SCENES FROM THE CLASSROOM

The assignment for the students was to read the case of Donald Marshall,[1] the young Micmac Indian who was accused and tried for murder in Nova Scotia. The case reflects the way in which racism played a strong part in Marshall's conviction. The teacher used the case as way of introducing the "big idea" of how racism shapes beliefs, attitudes, and behavior, to the detriment of the social weal.

To prepare for teaching the case, the teacher re-read it, and made several notes about what he wanted to highlight in his debriefing. He also made a list of the 5 questions he wanted to raise in getting at the big ideas. These higher-order questions were related to, but not the same as the ones at the end of the case. The questions would be his "prop" so that he could refer to them if needed during the discussions.

He had also prepared a list of follow-up activities for students to examine after their initial experiences with the case. These included several books (e.g., The Diary of Ann Frank; To Kill a Mockingbird; The Undefeated; Just Mercy*), and a few films (e.g.,* The Diary of Ann Frank; To Kill a Mockingbird; West Side Story; The Help; In the Heat of the Night; Mudbound*). These additional activities would also be followed by debriefing, so that various aspects of racist behavior would continue to be illuminated and examined.*

When the topic had been exploited to the teacher's satisfaction, the students would be asked to complete a project, done in pairs or small groups, that would reflect their growing understanding of the roots and implications of racism in our society.

In the brief scenario above the instructional design of teaching with cases is laid bare. It begins with the teacher's selection of the topic or the social issue that has been identified for extended study. In this case, the social issue was "the impact of racism on our thinking, attitudes, and behavior and the various ways in which racism undermines the most important values of a democratic society."

The case that the teacher chose was that of Donald Marshall, the Micmac Indian from Nova Scotia, who was charged and tried and convicted of murder. The case cites the many significant errors made in the trial, including the unprofessional conduct of the police in carrying out the investigation, the disregard of contrary evidence on the part of the primary detective, the lack of due diligence of the Crown prosecutor, and the many errors made by the trial judge, as well as the failure of the prosecution to disclose evidence that supported Marshall's innocence.

This case, then, was the introduction to the students' extended studies into the various elements of racism and its effect on many social systems in both Canada and the United States.

The Power of Cases to Teach the Big Ideas

From children's very early years, they are enchanted by stories. Bedtime stories are a staple in many homes, and it is not rare that children love to hear some of the same stories again and again, never tiring even though they already know every word.

In Robert Coles's book, *The Call of Stories* (1990), he describes how his own life has been impacted by stories that became beacons that inspired his professional life. "Stories," Cole wrote, "helped me to deal with patients, students, friends, and families in crisis; as readers connect with the characters in the stories, they are able to see the ethical considerations affecting the character's situation, and in that way, they learn about their responsibilities to themselves, friends and society and can make adjustments in their own lives."

In fact, Cole goes on to write, "our responses to the ethical questions found in stories make us who we are." Stories have great power—power to influence us in ways that many textbooks fail. That is perhaps because stories have both emotional and cognitive "weight" that allow us to identify with the characters. In a good story, we become those people. We feel with them; we care about them; they invade our thoughts and our hearts.

That is one reason why cases have such power to teach and to open minds to important issues in the ways that textbooks cannot. That is why they are such effective classroom teaching tools.

Small Group Work

There are good reasons to begin teaching with cases with small group work on the study questions. First and foremost is that small group discussions give students a chance to air their ideas, in a very safe context. No teacher is standing above them in judgment. No authority is listening to their perhaps, unfounded and erroneous assumptions. They are, in fact "practice sessions" to begin their serious conversations about the important issues. They are more than worth the time they consume and the efforts given to their effective functioning.

In these small study groups, students have a chance to listen to the ideas of their classmates and offer their own. The safer climate of these small groups makes it more comfortable for them to voice their ideas. It is also evident that these "practice sessions" in exploring ideas, responding, listening to other points of view, expressing one's own ideas are healthy preparations for what follows in the whole class discussions. Once having had the chance of "speaking one's mind," it is not so scary to offer one's ideas in view of the whole class. It also allows students practice in being able to articulate their ideas. Not a small gain.

Work in small study groups has direct pay off for the discussions in the more rigorous, whole class debriefing. Of course, it is also true that the challenging intellectual demands of debriefing implicitly impose standards of discourse in the small study groups. As well, the modeling of teacher-student interactions in the whole class debriefing also positively impacts the discussions in the small groups.

It doesn't necessarily follow that students immediately rise to the occasion if this is their first experience working in small study groups. Like most other learning opportunities, provision must be made to ensure that groups work effectively; that they are seriously engaged; that the discussions are productive. This is done by orienting the students to the nature of the experience—as teachers orient students to most new activities. Some ground rules are laid in preparation and it is helpful, of course, to enlist students' advice and recommendations for effective small group functioning. In that way, they assume agency over their behavior; it is not just behavior that is dictated by the teacher.

Some teachers create a poster on which guidelines for effective small group work are highlighted. In addition to suggestions by students, these would normally include references to behavior that was respectful, tolerance for the ideas of others, careful and attentive listening, and not interrupting. One such poster included:

- Listen carefully to each other's ideas.
- Work at trying to understand what is being said.
- Treat all students' ideas respectfully.
- Don't interrupt.
- Don't be a silent participant. Make sure you offer your own ideas.
- Raise questions when you don't understand. Ask for examples.
- Never put down another student for what he or she has said.
- Try to keep the discussion focused on the issues.

- During discussions, be alert to sweeping generalizations, personal judgments that pass as facts, extreme statements, simplistic conclusions, and conclusions that are not supported by data.

It is more than likely that small group discussions will not be effective immediately; it may take time for students to learn to work productively in these groups. In fact, this may be their very first opportunity at rising to these challenges. To become more effective, it is helpful at first, for the teacher to "attend" to the small group work by making his or her presence felt in moving from group to group, without intervention. Sometimes a teacher may wish to "sit in" on a group—again, without intervention.

Some teachers suggest a "post hoc" evaluation of how the groups worked—offering students a chance to comment and to make suggestions for improvement. It is often the case that when students have a chance to "weigh in" with their ideas, the application of those ideas to practice has a lot more power. Questions such as: How did the study groups work today? What procedures did you use to ensure productive discussions? How did the discussion get sidetracked? What ideas do you have for improving the functioning of the groups for next time?

It is essential for teachers conducting these post hoc evaluation sessions to remain neutral, allowing students to offer their views without judgment. Should teachers try to impeach students ideas, condemn suggestions, be sarcastic in their comments, or in any way undermine or devalue students statements, the process of reflective examination is doomed.

There may be instances of groups that have more difficulty staying on task; or those that require more direction; or those who have dysfunctional members. Should that be the case, a teacher's direct intervention may be required.

With appropriate interventions when necessary, with ample opportunities to examine group functioning in post hoc sessions, with continual modeling of effective teacher-student interactions in debriefing, the results in small group work should be clearly observable.

The Interactive Process of Debriefing a Case

Much has been written about the key feature of teaching with cases—the "debriefing"—or as it is sometimes called "teaching a case" (Christensen and Hansen, 1987; Ewing, 1990; Wassermann, 1994), each with its own spin on the process and each with its own perspectives. But the bottom line for all is that when "teaching a case" goes well, when it is done with the art and craft of a skilled teacher, the benefits to students are immense. Ewing (1990) has suggested that "it takes students out of the role of passive absorbers and makes them partners in the joint process of learning and furthering learning."

Ewing (1990) goes on to claim that "students learn to draw more fully upon each other's ideas in working out problems. Ideas and possible solutions come from everywhere, giving active listening an importance it could not have otherwise." Students learn to listen to each other, as well as to the teacher.

Done well, case discussions give students opportunities to grow from a "childlike dependence on teachers and parents to a state of dependable self reliance" (Gragg, 1940). But make no mistake: the discipline of the case method of learning is a not a walk in the park. Students are called upon to play active roles in processing information, in responding with intelligence and insight, making meaning from complex and sometimes uncertain situations. They learn to listen to each other's ideas, build on them, make decisions and offer ideas based on the facts in their possession. Volunteering one's ideas, at the outset, is intimidating, scary, daunting. It takes some time before students begin to feel safe in that kind of venue.

Much of the success of teaching with cases rests on the shoulders of the teacher. At the outset, the teacher sets the stage for what "debriefing" entails. This stage setting includes establishing a climate in which it is safe for students to offer their ideas. No matter how odd an idea may sound, it is treated with the same respectful attention that is offered to words of wisdom. Setting the stage also includes making students aware of the kinds of teacher-student interactions that will be used: reflective responses, responses calling for analyses, and responses that challenge students' thinking, in the absence of evaluative judgments.

Students may, at first, be put off by the teacher's nonjudgmental responses, where no student statement is evaluated. Each statement is, instead, used as "working material" in the dialogue between student and teacher, in the search for the important nuggets of thoughtfulness, the implicit and explicit meanings, the understanding of the big ideas. Instead of competition between students vying for the teacher's approval, for the "right answer," the students learn to listen to each other's ideas and use them as well for furthering understanding.

It is more than possible that students will, at first, feel "at sea" in a climate in which there are no right answers being sought and rewarded. So accustomed have they become to that kind of closure in a lesson, its absence may be unsettling, to say the least. Learning to live with that absence of closure, that uncertainty is one of the gifts of teaching with cases—because real life has few, if any, right answers. Learning to be comfortable with uncertainty opens the door for more introspection, for more suspended judgment, for the search for meaning.

The art and craft of debriefing, or of "teaching a case" lies in the teacher's skill in using the kinds of teacher-student interactions that ensure students' safety in offering their ideas, in listening carefully and attentively to students' statements, in responding reflectively so that students may re-examine what they have said, in using questions that call for students' analyses of their statements and in challenging them to re-think what has been said. Knowing when and how to use each of these responses is part of the teacher's growing skill in debriefing—and, alas, these skills are not simple applications, nor are they easily put to use.

The truth is that even the most skilled case teachers continue to examine and re-examine their debriefing skills over time, learning from each class, and making continuous inroads in their practice by that self-scrutiny. The good news is that even novices at the helm can't go far wrong when the intent and the self-scrutiny are foremost in the teacher's mind. Teaching then, becomes the "examined act."

But, in the end, it's more than worth the effort. The payoffs for teachers and students are unparalleled. That is why there is good reason for teachers to undertake such a professional journey.

Because the tools of the teacher-student interactive process are singular, a separate chapter, chapter 5, is devoted to what they involve and how they are used in teaching a case.

Creating a Climate for Serious Reflection

Before embarking on a more in-depth study of the teacher-student interaction skills, it may be a good idea to have a look at some of the underlying conditions that set the tone for a productive classroom discussion. Whichever questions and responses the teacher uses, certain aspects of "tone" contribute substantially to the ethos of the experience.

Inviting Rather Than Commanding

"Where on earth did you get that idea?" the teacher pounces. Her voice is raised, her finger pointed at the student under the gun. The student blanches, gulps, responds, "Aaaaaaagghhhrrrh," and slinks down into his seat, while others laugh. "It does them good," she says, defending her practice. "They know that they must support their ideas with data."

Of course students need to learn to reason with more logic, and one of the teacher's strategies to promote this more logical reasoning is to question, to probe, to ask the student to re-examine what has been said. But there are ways to do this that are more inviting, rather than more intimidating. This is not just an idle notion; more inviting responses are apt to get better replies. Students who are intimidated are more likely to feel defeated, frightened, and undermined.

So instead of asking with a thinly disguised reproach, it is more effective to turn the question into an invitation. For example:

Tell me a little more about how you figured that out. Or,
You may have some data to back up your idea. Or,
Can you give me an example of how that would work in practice?

It doesn't take any more effort to invite, instead of demand. In the responses that invite, students are still encouraged to reason from the data, but they are also treated with respect. In such a teacher-student partnership, where both are engaging in the process of finding out more, there is no room for the arrogant and authoritarian commands of a teacher.

Remaining Neutral

It is an almost innate response, born from many years listening to our own teachers:

"That's good, Jaime."
"Yes, that's an interesting idea, Ralph."
"You are making an important comment here and I'd like everyone to take note of it."
"Not quite right, Freda."

Evaluative responses fall from teachers' lips as easily as reciting abc's. And it is as hard to shed as a favorite pair of worn out slippers. But evaluative responses are anathema to a climate of serious inquiry for several reasons.

They torque the inquiry to "right answers"—those that are rewarded by the teacher's judgment.
They make "answers" the objective of the inquiry.
Students' responses are tilted toward getting teacher approval rather than toward the examination of issues.
They tend to shut down the discussion, rather than opening it for further study.

These are some important reasons that they be put aside during the process of debriefing a case.

If teachers doubt the effectiveness of dropping the evaluative response, they need only to look at some students' responses when they experience a more open discussion. (See, for example, students' comments in chapter 3).

Letting go of the judgment does not mean being unappreciative of students' ideas. But there is a wide gulf between "Good idea, Melvin" and "Thanks for letting us hear your ideas, Sophie."

Being Consistently Respectful

Respecting students and their ideas is, perhaps, one of the greatest gifts that teachers can offer students. Being respectful means taking students and their ideas seriously. It means listening to what they have to say with courtesy. It means treating them as you would guests in your home.

It's not enough for teachers to say, "I respect my students." Respect is seen in behavior; it is seen in how teachers treat students. To treat students respectfully means using invitations, instead of commands. It means freeing oneself from the role of authority when responding to students' ideas and opinions. It means avoiding making positive or negative judgments about students' responses. It means being flexible and open and nondefensive in the presence of student challenges. To behave in ways that are truly respectful of students and their ideas requires a predisposition to the idea that students deserve respect. When such behavior is exhibited in case discussions, the results can be powerful.

Respect given is respect earned.

Watching for the Effect

"What do you think happened to the dinosaurs?" she asks. She watches Harold as he hears the question; there is the briefest raising of the eyebrows and a shutting down. "I don't know," he answers with an emphasis on the "I"—as if to say, "How do you expect me to know that?" The effect of her question teaches her something important: The question is too challenging. Harold may be hearing it as a call for the right answer. He has resisted coming up with even a single idea.

Given her "reading" of his response, she is able to repair the damage.

"I was wondering if you have any theories about it?" Introducing the word "theories" opens up some possibilities for him. He doesn't have to know the answer. He is being invited to conjecture.

"Well," he offers, "I think they might have gotten killed off by some disease." He is beginning to formulate his theory. The idea is to keep the thinking line open.

"How could that happen, I wonder? Could you help me to understand?" At this invitation he begins to expand on his "dinosaur-disease" theory in which an epidemic might have killed off this species. He does have ideas to offer, given the right conditions. If the "wheels begin to turn," he will even venture to give them. His theory may be naïve, but at least he has taken the risk to offer one. A first step.

It would not be an exaggeration to state that every question a teacher asks, every response a teacher makes, has both cognitive and affective power. Learning to "read and interpret" that effect is an immensely valuable skill in making it safe for students to offer their ideas and in building a climate of safety and trust. A look of bewilderment may be mitigated by, "Perhaps I didn't make my question clear. Let me ask that in another way."

For a student who fails to respond, a teacher might offer: "That was a tough question. You may want some time to think about it. Let me know when you want me to get back to you." A student's response that is confusing might be helped with: "Help me to understand. I'm losing the thread of what you are trying to tell me."

The interactive dialogue is not a game in which the teacher is the hunter and the student the prey. It is a partnership in which teacher and student engage in an examination of ideas, leading to more intelligent meaning making. The teacher who is able to apprehend fully and be cognitively and affectively aware of the many nuances in the interactive process will be able to draw on those resources to the benefit of both and of the inquiry process.[2]

Follow-Up Activities

From the many and varied experiences that teachers have had with case method teaching, one obvious result is that an effectively taught case drives the need to know more. The case itself just sets the stage and generates interest in the issues. Debriefing further heightens the tension. Both of these processes contribute to students' motivation to inquire further—to "fill in the blanks," satisfy their curiosity, and obtain additional information and supporting data.

In teaching with cases, answers are not "found." Instead, ambiguities are exposed and tension increases. Consequently, the need to know becomes more urgent. Here, then is the motivation for knowledge building. The teacher does not dispense information; the students' need to know opens the door to knowledge acquisition.

Some cases come with a list of follow-up activities; teachers may also generate their own list. In the latter case, social studies textbooks and other related references may provide more than could ever be studied for one case. In other words, there is no dearth of options for follow-up experiences. Among these would be text materials, films, videos, photographs, editorials, magazine articles, tables and charts, newspapers, field trips, and other supplements. Novels are another good source of supplementary material.

Follow-up activities may be carried out individually, or in pairs or small groups. Students should, however, be able to make their own choices with respect to what follow-up activity they wish to pursue. Whatever follow-up activities are used, their value is increased by further debriefing-like discussions in which the big ideas get extended examination and new perspectives are introduced. Through this process, students' thoughtful, critical examination of the significant issues continually evolves.

At this point, teachers may ask: But how long does this process take? How long for the introduction of the case, the study groups, the debriefing and the follow up? As in many things a teacher does, it depends. Some cases plus follow-up activities will warrant longer exposure because the issues have greater impact for the students and their need to know more has not yet been satisfied. Other cases may not have the same power and therefore, the case plus follow-up may be shorter lived.

The teacher is always the best judge of time allocation and given that, in most classrooms the curriculum to be studied is always at war with the clock, a case or any curriculum experience will never be completely wrung dry. Teachers already know that there is never enough time to do justice to all the issues; never enough time to debrief all the follow-up activities; never enough time to teach everything. Learning to live with that "unfinished business" is one of the frustrating aspects of a teacher's life. If it's any comfort, however, the data suggest that students will continue to think about the case long after the classroom door closes.

END NOTES

Teachers who use case method teaching effectively have been excited about the results they see in their students: students learn to communicate their ideas more effectively; they learn to examine complicated issues in more thoughtful ways. Their curiosity is aroused and their interest in learning is increased. Students also show more respect for different ideas, different attitudes, different points of view, different beliefs held by other students. They are more motivated to read more and learn more about what's important.

Teachers have also found that discussions begun in class carry over to the lunch room and the school yard and also to the dinner table at home.

There are good reasons to believe that effectively carried out, case method teaching is a methodology for all seasons.

NOTES

1. A copy of the Case of Donald Marshall is found in Chapter 6. Permission is given for it to be duplicated for classroom use.

2. Adapted by permission of the Publisher. From Selma Wassermann, *Introduction to Case Method Teaching: A Guide to the Galaxy*. New York: Teachers College Press. Copyright © 1994 by Teachers College, Columbia University. All rights reserved.

Chapter 5

The Tools of the Interactive Process

SCENES FROM THE CLASSROOM

It was the grade 7 students' first experience with case method teaching. They had prepared the case, "A Conflict of Cultures" (McNeill, 1991) that dealt with newly arrived immigrants facing many conflicts in their new country. They were now ready for their first debriefing session.

The students were eager to continue the discussion as the case seemed to have hit a chord with them, raising issues that brought home some of their own values and concerns. In preparation for the whole class discussion the teacher began by outlining her protocols:

I know that this method of discussion may be different for you and I'd like to give you some guidelines for making the discussion more productive. First, I'd like you all to be as respectful and attentive as possible to the ideas that anyone is presenting.

Second, my strategy will be to call on someone who has their hand up and I will work with that student's ideas. At any time during that discussion, that student may tell me, "That's enough!" In other words, each student may end the discussion with me; no problem.

Third, I won't call on anyone who doesn't have a hand up. I will only call on volunteers.

Fourth, I will not be telling you that your idea is good or bad or wrong or right. I will only work with your idea to help bring more clarity to the issues.

At the end of the discussion it is more than possible that the issues will not be resolved and all questions answered to your satisfaction. That may give you a chance to follow up, read and discuss more, and perhaps even have another whole class discussion. Before we begin, does anyone have any questions about these procedures?

Preparing for the Debriefing

The day before debriefing the case, Stella Lee made her preparations by reviewing the case. She made certain that the big ideas, outlined in the Notes to the Teacher were at the forefront of her mind. She was clear that the points of emphasis would be the reasons why immigrants choose to move from their birth countries and embark on new lives in "foreign" lands, and the difficulties they face in making their adjustments to their new countries. Some of these difficulties include facing intolerance from neighbors, the conflicts between wanting to preserve some of their old culture and the press of the new culture on old habits and mores, and the problems arising in making these accommodations.

In her study of the case, Stella used a highlighter to mark certain facts, so that these would be fresh in her mind during the debriefing, to spare herself any meltdown during what invariably occurs when the discussion gets heated. She also read again the chapter in the social studies textbook that dealt with immigration from an historical and a more current perspective.

Then, using the big ideas of the case, the case narrative, and the study questions as a springboard, Stella began to formulate some of the challenging social issues she would be raising during the discussion. These included:

The many and diverse reasons people choose to leave their mother countries and seek homes in foreign lands.
The many and diverse problems faced by new immigrants as they begin their lives in their adopted countries.
The tension in families between immigrant adults who want to retain some of their old culture and mores and immigrant youth who are more eager to embrace the new culture.
The roots of intolerance toward immigrants.

Debriefing the Case

Once the students had settled down to start the discussion, Stella began by asking for a volunteer to present an overview of the case.

> Teacher: Who would like to begin by telling us what this case is about?
>
> (The teacher waits for what seems a long time. Some students snicker. Some look up at the ceiling. Some fix their eyes on the clock. The teacher continues to wait. Then, finally . . .) Yes, Barry.
>
> Barry: Well, this case was about a family who just moved to Canada from Sweden. I think this was a long time ago and not recently. They are having a

hard time adjusting to the new country. They are not able to grow crops on their farm and the adults have to go to work on the railroad to make money. They had to leave Sweden because the father was running away from the police. They were starving.

Teacher: Thank you Barry for opening the discussion. I appreciate it. Let me see if I can make something clearer. In your summary of the case you say that this family left Sweden because they were running from the police. Could you explain that a little more?

Barry: Okay. They were starving so the father shot a deer which was against the law. And that is why they had to escape. So it wasn't as if they were murderers or something like that.

Teacher: Killing a deer because you are hungry is not in the same category as murder. You don't think that's so bad.

Barry: Yes, that's not so bad if you are starving.

Teacher: Thank you Barry for giving us your ideas and thank you again for opening the discussion. Barry has mentioned one reason that the family had to immigrate. Does anyone else want to comment about their reasons for leaving Sweden?

(More hands are now in the air.)

Debbie: Well in those days they lived on land that belonged to the land owner. And they didn't own land of their own. So what they had really belonged to someone else and they didn't have anything. They had no food. So when the father shot the deer, the police went after him. He would have landed in jail. So they had to flee.

Teacher: Debbie I may be reading something more into what you are telling us—but I'm getting the idea, from what you are saying, that you think that what happened to the father was unjust.

Debbie: Well I think that if everything you have belongs to the land owner, and you have to obey his rules, even if you are starving, that's very wrong.

Teacher: You are perhaps seeing an important reason for the family to have left Sweden and fleeing to another country. To be safe? To have more opportunity? To not have to be at the mercy of the land owner?

Debbie: Yes, all of that.

Teacher: Thanks Debbie. I'd like to raise another question now and that is what happened to the family when they moved to Canada. What were some of the problems they faced?

In this brief scenario are seen the key elements of teaching a case. At first the teacher explains the protocols for discussion and makes them clear. Then, she invites responses to her first question and waits until someone is brave enough to open the dialogue. She uses reflective responses that mirror the student's statement, giving students the chance to reconsider what they have said—as the idea is being played back to them. This demonstrates how carefully the teacher is listening and how she respects what the student has said.

Once she is satisfied that her initial question has been addressed by several student responses, she moves to her first challenging question. Reflective responses are the core, the bedrock responses in debriefing. These are followed by carefully chosen questions that call for analysis of the big ideas and questions that challenge students' thinking. The objective is to allow students to explain what they understand, to clarify their thinking, and to open new lines of inquiry. These ideas are put under scrutiny in the most respectful way possible.

Cold Calls

In the above scenario, the teacher waits until students volunteer to offer their ideas. She doesn't call on students who have not raised a hand. In the parlance of case method teaching, this is termed "cold calling." At higher levels of instruction, like graduate schools of business, cold calling is a mainstay of a case discussion. The underlying principle is that all students must be fully and exhaustively prepared if they receive the "nod" from the teacher to respond.

It is obvious even to the uninitiated that cold calling puts a heavy onus on students and creates more than a minimum amount of anxiety in the class. It puts students on edge; and in some instances, in terror of being called. Yet, some teachers believe that such anxiety leads to better preparedness and they will not be persuaded otherwise.

In the end, it is a matter of a teacher's preference, whether to use cold calling in a debriefing or whether to wait for volunteers.

Yet, in a classroom where one of the values is the teacher's respect for the students, cold calling cannot fit into that ethos. The creation of anxiety in students is not what is considered a healthy element in a classroom climate.

The Interactive Tools of a Case Discussion

Teachers who have studied the art of interactive teaching have identified several skills used in concert to bring students' ideas under examination. These are not all the skills used by a discussion leader, but they seem to be the ones considered basic for a successful discussion. In debriefing a case, the teacher does the following:

- Listens, attends, and apprehends students' statements

- Comprehends the message the student is giving
- Selects from a range of options the type of response to be made, with full appreciation that different responses have different cognitive and affective effects
- Chooses higher-order questions that put the big ideas of the case under examination
- Raises questions that promote cognitive dissonance

These responses do not follow any specific sequence but are used selectively, in each interaction, moving smoothly and seamlessly in a provocative examination of issues. This orchestration of responses is at the heart of effective discussion teaching.

Listening, Attending, Apprehending

To make a pudding you need to add the ingredients one by one and blend them smoothly into the batter. To orchestrate a debriefing, you need to listen, attend, and apprehend what each student is saying, what is being communicated both in spoken words, and in the messages between the lines. You need to apprehend the body language as well. Taking all of that into account gives the teacher the data on which to formulate a response.

Carkhuff and Berenson (1983) were the first among several authors who pointed to the essential conditions that contribute to effective listening, attending and apprehending. These include:

- Making and holding eye contact with the student speaking
- Listening to and communicating respect for the student's idea
- Being free from the need to evaluate the student's idea in either word or tone
- Avoiding reactive comments on the student's idea; avoiding offering one's own thoughts
- Apprehending: making meaning of what the student is saying
- Being aware of tone of affect, verbal or nonverbal
- Being especially aware of indicators of stress
- Formulating responses that accurately and sensitively reflect the meaning of the student's statement
- Being able to make the student feel safe, nondefensive, nonthreatened in the dialogue

These conditions—the ability to listen, apprehend, and attend provides the teacher with the information needed to formulate appropriate responses. They create the climate in which respect for students and for their ideas is self-evident. They make it safe for students to think their own thoughts and to present them for analysis.

When all of that is present, teacher and students become engaged in a dialogue in a search for clearer understanding. The teacher's skill in listening, attending, and apprehending is the indispensable tool in the art of debriefing. It is upon this foundation that the other skills rest.

Selecting a Response

For teachers looking for the formula for choosing the "right" response to a student's statement at the "right" moment in the discourse, these next paragraphs will not make them best pleased. For there is no formula, no specific paradigm, no explicit "key" that says: first this, then this, then that. While that may, at first, be discouraging, there is a certain liberty to it—the liberty that teachers have to use their own judgment to come up with the best response at the right moment.

There are dozens of ways in which teachers respond to students. They may choose to agree or disagree. They may offer their own ideas, give explanations, provide examples, give information. Responses may be directive or judgmental. Even no response is a response of a kind. None of these, however, has much to do with the kinds of responses teachers may use to bring students' ideas under examination. That is not to say that such responses are wrong or never used. They are appropriate in other contexts but singularly inappropriate in debriefing a case.

In debriefing a case, there are three increasingly more challenging categories of responses (Wassermann, 2009): basic responses that encourage students' re-examination of their ideas; responses that call for analysis of their ideas; and responses that challenge. Each of these is used selectively and as appropriate in the interactive dialogue.

Basic Responses That Encourage Students' Re-examination of Their Ideas

Basic responses are fundamental to the interactive process. While called "basic," this should not be interpreted as having less power to promote thoughtful reflection. The power they do have is to communicate to the student that his or her idea has been heard. They "play back" the idea in some new way, putting up a verbal mirror so that the student has an opportunity to re-examine it from a fresh perspective.

Students who are habituated to this "playing back" of their statements learn, over time, to take greater responsibility for what is coming out of their mouth. Implicit in this is that what they have said is going to be listened to and used as "working material." A student may have to think twice before uttering irresponsible statements. This is hardly a small gain.

Basic responses are minimally challenging; as a consequence, students feel safer to respond. Liberally used they build trust in the relationship and do the basic work of promoting reflection. These responses include:

- Saying the idea back to the student in some new way
- Paraphrasing the idea
- Interpreting the idea
- Asking for more information (e.g., "Tell me a little more about that," or "Help me to understand what you mean.")

The more closely a teacher's response mirrors what a student has said, the less challenge it creates. However, basic responses do not move the inquiry into deeper examinations. Those calling for more intensive probing are those that require analysis or those that challenge—both categories are more risky, in terms of cognitive challenges, for the student. The artful teacher must balance the scale between responses that make it safe for the student to re-examine a statement and responses that challenge the student's thinking.

There is no pattern that teachers can follow in making those choices. This is why listening, attending, and apprehending pay off. They give teachers the data from which they can choose the most appropriate response.

The good news is that a basic response is never wrong. It may not serve the purpose of probing deeply but it is an effective tool in asking students to re-examine and take responsibility for their ideas. Teachers should not underestimate the power of basic responses to promote students' examination of their ideas.

One caveat about using these basic responses is to avoid falling into the trap of using the same kind of statement again and again. These kinds of repetitive responses become formulaic and mechanical, rather than productive. They are indicators that the teacher has not listened, attended, and apprehended—using what a student has said to bring him or her to a better awareness of his or her idea.

When teachers are able to free their minds from making judgments of students' statements, from offering their own ideas, from giving examples, from supplying information—those standard responses in a teacher's repertoire, they are more able to listen, attend, and apprehend, making the task of choosing a response more accessible.

RESPONSES THAT CALL FOR ANALYSIS OF AN IDEA

At a slightly more challenging level than basic responses are those that call for analysis of ideas. These responses require deeper thought and go beyond surface observations. These include:

- Asking that examples be given
- Asking whether assumptions are being made
- Asking whether alternatives have been considered
- Asking whether alternatives have been considered
- Asking for supporting data
- Asking where the idea came from

This is not an exhaustive list, but they give an idea of the kind of responses that raise the level of challenge for the student. As it can be seen, each moves beyond the obvious of what has been said, asking that the student dig more deeply into what lies behind the statements. Also, unlike basic responses that are framed as declarative sentences, responses that call for analysis are usually framed as questions. They are considered more challenging because they pose greater risks for the student, who has to defend ideas with supporting data.

One important criterion for choosing a question that calls for analysis is to make certain that the question is going to add an important new dimension to the examination of issues. Questions are never chosen haphazardly; they are rather chosen by the teacher after reflection on their potential to move the discussion toward greater understanding. One way to make these queries slightly less challenging is to frame them as declaratives, rather than as questions. For example:

Instead of "What examples can you give to support that idea?" try, "Perhaps you have some examples that you can give us."
Instead of "What assumptions have you made?" try, "You might be making some assumptions here. I wonder what they might be."
Instead of "Where did you get that idea?" try "I'm wondering if you have had that idea for a long time."

Invitations to respond, rather than questions, are likely to make the student feel safer to respond, even when called upon to dig for deeper meanings.

The vortex of debriefing, where a dozen students' hands are in the air, when the teacher is trying to keep track of what has been said and of where the discourse is going, trying to focus on the big ideas and bring them under careful scrutiny, is a challenge for even the most experienced case teachers.

In such a climate, it is easy to fall back on more familiar and widely used questions, such as "Why do you think so?" or "Why or Why not?" These, however, should be avoided if at all possible. They not only challenge inappropriately but are not sharply focused. If the intent is to promote clearer understanding of the big ideas, it's best to leave "why" questions to another venue.

RESPONSES THAT CHALLENGE AT HIGHER COGNITIVE LEVELS

At the most demanding level of the cognitive scale is that group of questions that require the generation of new ideas. These ask students to extend their thinking into new territories, to come up with ideas that go beyond what has been seen or heard; to take data and manipulate them into new configurations, so that something new is revealed. These questions put students at the highest cognitive risk. Understandably, they are used sparingly during debriefing. They include:

- Asking that hypotheses be generated
- Asking that data be interpreted
- Asking that principles be applied to new situations
- Asking that evaluations be made and criteria be identified
- Asking that predictions be made about what is theoretically possible
- Asking how new theories might be tested
- Asking that plans of action be created
- Asking that decisions be made and their consequences examined

These do not exhaust the list of what might be asked. However, they give an idea of the kinds of questions that constitute such challenges as well as demonstrating the difficulty of what is being asked.

Teachers who are new to debriefing often make the mistake of thinking that challenging questions run the show in good discussion teaching. That however is not the case. Challenging questions are merely one tool in the teacher's response toolkit. Like hammers, which are no better tools in the abstract than screwdrivers, invaluable when used effectively, and with the potential of causing harm when used ineffectively, the tools of challenging questions are best used with the following caveats in mind.

Challenging questions, by their very nature, shift the discourse onto new pathways. A result of using several challenging questions in succession is that the discussion begins to appear fractured and disjointed, as each idea is immediately abandoned for a new idea. It is the basic response that grounds the discussion and permits a slower, more studied examination. Challenging questions need to be used thoughtfully, sparingly, and wisely, and only when the teacher wishes to shift the inquiry onto a new plane.

Another caveat regarding challenging questions is that they pose a greater cognitive risk in asking students to respond. They may frustrate students and cause them to feel "stupid." This should be a red flag to teachers who may fall into the trap of using challenging questions indiscriminately.

Challenging questions when used, may be "softened" by posing them as invitations, rather than as cognitive demands. Students may feel less intimidated when asked, "You may have some hypotheses to explain that," rather than, "What hypotheses do you have to explain that?"[1]

Orchestrating a Debriefing Session

In the 1930s during the Great Depression, industries went bankrupt, farmers suffered great hardships, there was a loss of export markets, and unemployment rose to staggering proportions. Loss of employment meant no income, hunger, despair, loss of hope, loss of homes, and loss of human dignity—for families and individuals. More than 20 million people lost their jobs in the U.S. and in Canada, more than 10 million people were on the relief rolls.

In the "Case of Swallowed Pride" (Wassermann, 1991), a farming family who has lost everything, must reach out to social services for help. Because their need is so great, they must overcome their shame in asking for this help.

The teacher's goals are not only to raise awareness of the immensity of the problems during the Great Depression on lives, and on the loss of hope, but also to juxtapose this in relation to what happened during the 2020–2021 COVID-19 pandemic.

> Teacher: I wonder who would like to begin by giving us a brief summary of the case.
>
> Sean: I can start. This family was on a farm. Their crops had failed. They had to sell one of their horses. They had no money coming in and they were hungry. The mother wanted the daughter to go out and use the food vouchers to get food. But the girl was ashamed.
>
> Teacher: Thank you Sean for opening up the discussion. You are pointing to some of what happened during that time in the 1930s called the Great Depression. This family was destitute. They could get some help with food vouchers, but there was shame in asking for charity. (*Places the event in the time called The Great Depression, which Sean had omitted and reflects the substance of Sean's statement.*)

The Tools of the Interactive Process 41

Sean: Yeh. The case made me feel bad for what the family was feeling.

Teacher: You were identifying with the family and their harsh situation. (*Reflects*)

Sean: Nods.

Teacher: Thanks, Sean. I'd like to ask now what you know about the Great Depression of the 1930s.

Annie: From this case and what I've been reading, I remember that it was a time of great hardship. People lost their jobs. Companies went bankrupt. Some families had nothing. It was a terrible time.

Teacher: Your readings of the case and of other material gave you some feeling about the time when banks failed, companies closed, and there was tremendous unemployment. (*Paraphrases and adds a statement about the banks.*)

Annie: In the case, the mother sent her daughter, I think her name was Sarah, to the store with food vouchers. The mother was ashamed to go herself and the daughter was ashamed too. But she had to go.

Teacher: There is some sense of being ashamed to have to accept charity when you are hungry and have nothing. (*Paraphrases*)

Annie: I don't understand that. If you are hungry, why not just accept the food, if it is available.

Teacher: If it was you, you wouldn't be ashamed to take the food if you were desperate. (*Interprets*)

Annie: Nods.

Teacher: Thanks, Annie. I want to raise another question now. From your readings and your understanding of this historic event, what do you suppose were some of the conditions that led to this epic economic failure? (*Raises a challenging question by asking for hypotheses*)

Lowell: I think it had something to do with the stock market, but I'm not sure how that works. But I do remember that stocks that were worth a lot of money suddenly were worth nothing.

Teacher: You see it as something that was brought about by the failure at the stock market. (*Reflects*)

Lowell: That's beyond me. I don't understand how these things work, but I do know that people were jumping out of windows and committing suicide because their stocks were worthless and they lost everything.

Teacher: It's a complicated situation to know what actually happened on Wall Street—but you believe it had something to do with how stocks lost their value. And people who were ruined committed suicide. (*Paraphrases*) So can you give some examples of how the government helped? (*Raises a related question by asking for supporting data*)

Pru: Well, like in the case, there were food vouchers. The family could use them to get food for free at the shop.

Teacher: Food vouchers were one way in which the government stepped in to help those in need. (*Reflects*) How did that work, do you suppose? (*Challenges by asking for hypotheses*)

Pru: The case tells you that it was not all good. Because you had to humble yourself to accept charity. And for some people that was hard.

Teacher: Accepting charity is not easy for some people. It may say something about them? (*Reflects and challenges by asking for hypotheses*)

Marvelle: Well it's okay for some people. They don't care. They'll take any hand out they can get. But for some people, it's humiliating.

Teacher: People respond in different ways to accepting charity. (*Paraphrases*) For some, it's easy. For others, it's humiliating. (*Paraphrases*) Can you say a little more about why it would be humiliating, Marvelle? (*Challenges; asks for hypotheses*)

Marvelle: I'm not sure. I think it might have something to do with pride. It says something about you if you are so desperate you need to get food from the food bank or from vouchers.

Teacher: It may be pride that makes a person feel ashamed to accept charity. (*Paraphrases*)

I'd like to ask some more questions about what happened during the Great Depression, besides what you read in the case. (*Challenges; asks for additional data about the period*)

Brenda: Well I know many people lost their jobs and there were no new jobs to find, because so many businesses closed. Even those who had businesses that were open did not make a lot of money because people didn't have a lot to spend.

Teacher: What you are describing is like a domino effect—businesses closed and people lost their jobs. They couldn't find other jobs. And the businesses that were open couldn't make a lot of profit because people didn't have any money to spend. One thing led to another in a chain reaction. (*Interprets*)

Artie: Yeh a chain reaction. Like a downward spiral that couldn't be stopped. It just went from bad to worse.

Teacher: So given this downward spiral that just kept getting worse, (*Paraphrases*) how did people manage? How did they get through those years? (*Challenges; asks for hypotheses*)

Peter: It gives me the creeps to think about it. I don't know how they managed. It must have been a terrible time.

Teacher: Somehow some people did manage—but it was a terrible time for everyone. (*Paraphrases*) I'd like to bring these ideas a bit closer in time and ask you to think about how people managed in another crisis time—the COVID-19 pandemic of 2020–2021. (*Challenges; asks that the principles of "managing" be applied to more recent events*)

The discussion continues in this fashion until the teacher reaches her end point—by asking about the impact on the human condition when people have to endure years of hardship, comparing the Great Depression to the events during COVID-19 and how a government may step up to provide needed help. As part of the follow-up activities students will be reading supplementary resource materials, e.g., *The Grapes of Wrath*, *Let Us Now Praise Famous Men*, and *Hard Times* as well as viewing films, e.g., *The Grapes of Wrath*, *Sullivan's Travels*, *Between Two Wars*, *Modern Times*, *Of Mice and Men*, *Places in the Heart*, *The Color Purple*.

END NOTES

There is an art to successful debriefing—much like the maestro conducting Mahler's *Resurrection* Symphony. Knowing when to cue in the violins, the winds, the chorus; knowing when to call for forte or piano; knowing which melodic line is to be heard above the rest of the sounds—all of that combining to make beautiful music. None of that happens in a single session. Sometimes it takes years for a maestro to perfect his or her skill. And it should also be pointed out that different maestros have different interpretations of the same piece of music.

Likewise, different teachers are more than likely to orchestrate a debriefing session of the same case with different emphases. That is just the way it works.

The art of debriefing is not learned in one session; it is a cumulative process. One learns to do better from reflecting on what has occurred and making suggestions to self for the next time. Yes, wrong notes will be heard and the timpani will be cued too soon. Yes, the teacher will use too many challenging questions and perhaps insert a "why" question inappropriately. Yes, the nature of the exploration of the big ideas may go off track. This is the price of learning the art. One can't be perfect every time; one can't be perfect at the first trial. Expecting that of oneself is the pathway to defeatism.

NOTE

1. Adapted by permission of the Publisher. From Selma Wassermann, *Introduction to Case Method Teaching: A Guide to the Galaxy*. New York: Teachers College Press. Copyright © 1994 by Teachers College, Columbia University. All rights reserved.

Chapter 6

Cases Based on Critical Issues in the Social Studies

The ten cases included in this chapter come with permission for teachers to duplicate them and distribute them as teaching materials to their students. Each case begins with the identification of the "big ideas" on which the case rests, the study questions for use in small group work, and a list of options for follow-up activities. In other words, each case can function as a complete curriculum unit on the particular social issue being studied.

The cases touch on the following social issues:

Disinformation and the Internet
Racism and its impact on immigration
The Civil Rights Bill and the integration of public schools
Pollution and the environment
Choosing a candidate
The justice system and racism
The Spanish Flu and COVID-19
Some problems facing new immigrants
Income disparity
Human relationships and community

CASE 1: "I READ IT ON THE INTERNET"

Notes to the Teacher: This case is concerned with the topic of disinformation, how it is spread, how it is accepted as "truth" and what the implications are of the spread of false and malicious data to persuade the naïve and vulnerable to accept lies as reality.

The big ideas that shape the case are:

1. "Information" comes from various sources, some of which are deliberately torqued to present a particular point of view.
2. Separating out truth from disinformation has become a skill requiring cognitive awareness, suspension of judgment, and critical reasoning.
3. In listening to or watching the news, it important to be able to verify that what we are hearing is truth rather than alternate truth.
4. Acting on disinformation is very likely to cause us to behave in ways that are irrational, weird, and even dangerous.

Case: I Read It on the Internet

Sara was thrilled with her new cell phone. She had wanted one for her birthday and her mom and dad came through and bought her a pink one. It had messaging, art, and mapping apps, videos, games—and she could even do FaceTime. Her phone would also allow her to connect with Twitter. She was over the moon!

The first thing she did on that Saturday morning was to sign on to Twitter and see what messages her friends were sending. Reading and answering them took a big part of her morning. It was a beautiful spring day, the weather was warm, and she would have probably gone outside if she wasn't stuck to her phone. Never mind. Having this private link to the World Wide Web was much more interesting.

As she was scrolling down, up popped a new e-mail from Walt Disney, Jr.! Wow! This was thrilling. In the message, Disney said that if she would forward the e-mail to as many friends as possible and if it reached 13,000 people, the first 1,300 would receive a gift of $5,000 and the rest would get a free trip for two to Disney World. All you had to do was to send in your entry fee of $10.00. Sara had that much and more in her savings account. This was easy!

She couldn't wait to tell her friends.

On Monday, at school during the lunch break, she talked to her group of best friends about the Disney e-mail and the exciting offer. All they needed to pay was $10.00 to enter. And they would be sure to get a free trip to Disney World.

At first, the girls were doubtful. How did Sara know this was true?

"I read it on the Internet," Sara said, pleased.

"But how do you know this is true?" said Melody.

"It was on the Internet."

The girls seemed satisfied. They would dip into their allowances and come up with the $10.00 entry fee. Then, all they had to do was wait for the message to reach 13,000 people and they would be off to Disney World. Wasn't the Internet wonderful that it could send you these exciting offers?

It didn't take Sara long to persuade a large group of her classmates to chip in with their $10.00 entry fees and send them off to the Internet site. Weeks passed. Then months. And still no word from Walt Disney, Jr. about their free trip to Disney World. Some of her friends began to question her and some actually accused her of being scammed. "We gave you our money and we trusted you. So where's our trip to Disney World?"

"But," Sara was close to weeping. "Maybe they still didn't get 13,000 people. Maybe that's why we haven't heard. If it was on the Internet it had to be true."

Study Questions

1. What do you see as the important features of this case? How would you summarize the case in two sentences?
2. What do you suppose was in the message from Walt Disney, Jr. that made Sara believe it was true?
3. What might Sara have done to check to see if the offer from Disney was a scam? What are your ideas about it?
4. Why do you suppose it's so easy to fall for information that comes on the Internet? What hypotheses can you give to explain it?
5. What are some of the best ways to find out if information is true or false? What are your ideas about it?
6. In your opinion, what might be some of the dangers of the misinformation that comes from the Internet?

Follow-Up Activities

https://www.theitalianexperiment.com/stories/chichen-little (N.B. Although the story is written in Italian, it is also available in translation in this same site.)
Chang, Juju and Dubreuil. 2009. *Abducted by Aliens*
https://abcnews.go.com/Primetime/story?id=83302903
Pattison, Darcy & Willis, Peter. 2017. *The Nantucket Sea Monster*
Young-Brown, Fiona. 2019. *Fake News and Propaganda*
Doeden, Matt. 2019. *What are Hoaxes and Lies*?

CASE 2: "NONE IS TOO MANY!"

Notes to the Teacher: This case draws on the theme of racial prejudice and does so in the context of the plight of the Jews in Germany during World War

II. The case centers on a single event, the departure in 1939 of 936 Jews from Hamburg, on the German ship, the *St. Louis*, bound for Havana, with paid-for Cuban "landing certificates" that would allow them to enter Cuba legally. Many of the Jews who were embarking for Cuba as a safe haven had already had members of their families taken away to concentration camps. Their immigration to a country outside of Germany meant, for all, the difference between life and death.

Because of anti-Jewish sentiment in Cuba and because of behind-the-scenes corruption in the granting of the Jewish "landing certificates," the Cuban officials chose not to honor them, and invalidated them. When Captain Schroeder radioed this news back to Germany, he received explicit instructions for the ship, which sailed under the German flag, to return to Germany at once. This, he knew, meant certain death for the refugees. In a heroic effort, he attempted to contact other countries, pleading for permission to allow his passengers to enter. Both the United States and Canada refused permission. Immigration laws in both countries excluded people who were considered "undesirable."

Without any other option, Captain Schroeder set sail for Germany on June 5.

In what was truly a last-minute rescue, the captain learned that Great Britain, the Netherlands, Belgium, and France had each agreed to take a share of the passengers. The passengers drew lots, to determine which families were to go where. Two hundred and eighty-seven went to England; 214 went to Belgium; 224 went to France, and 181 went to the Netherlands.

Of these, most who went to Belgium, France, and the Netherlands later became victims of the "Final Solution," when Germany invaded and occupied these countries.

The big ideas on which this case rests are:

1. Racial hatred was responsible for the murder of six million men, women, and children in Germany and its occupied countries during the Nazi regime.
2. Identifying a particular group as "undesirable" or "less" allows us to treat them in less than human ways.
3. Immigration laws are often designed to keep "unwanted" people out of "first world" countries.
4. Racial hatred makes it possible for people to behave in ways that they would otherwise consider irrational, inhuman, aberrant, and evil.

Case: "None Is Too Many!"

They came when I was asleep, dreaming of better days. The pounding at the door woke me rudely. As I lay there with the covers over my face, I tried to see in the half-light what was going on. I heard my father go to the door and then the sound of voices, in high German, so cold they brought chills to my bones. The voices commanded my father to go with them and they took him away into the night, with only the clothes he had on when he answered the door. I heard my mother's cry, a long, painful wail, like an animal whose limb had been torn off. I crept out of my bed and saw my mother weeping, her head pressed against the door that had closed behind my father's departure.

I was eleven when the SS came to take my father. It was April 1, April Fools' Day. Only fools would have chosen to remain in Germany so long, you think? Foolish Jews who thought that any day things would get better; who thought that this nightmare couldn't really be happening in our wonderful country. But every day there were more signs of brutality against the Jews and we were constantly singled out for the most vicious attacks and humiliations. It became impossible even to walk down the street without fear that you would be spat upon, hit by a rock, or even worse, taken away never to be seen again.

Yet, some of us, in our very civilized and respectable city of Augsburg, in the heart of civilized Germany, still felt we were Germans. We were citizens of a great country, with a great literary, cultural, and artistic heritage. This was the birthplace of genius, of Beethoven, of Nietzsche, of Bach. How could such civilized people be doing this to us?

In the cold gray dawn of that early April morning, my mother sat us down at the kitchen table. Her ashen face told of her terror and we three children listened in stunned silence. My sister, Ilse, who was only five, hardly made sense of my mother's words, but even she could tell that this was bad. My other sister, Lotte was nine, and she and I were old enough to know there was real horror in this nightmare. My father had been taken by the SS, Hitler's special force of military elite, the guardians of "pure blood," who were trained to strike without fear or compassion.

Dressed in sleek black uniforms, with the fearful double zigzag insignia, they were the very essence of cold, calculated evil. Their special job was to preserve the pure Aryan blood of the true German people. Jews were "undesirables." They had to be eliminated to keep the race pure. The SS removal of my father was part of a larger plan to exterminate Jews in Germany and then, in all the other countries that were occupied by Hitler's advancing armies.

We had no way of knowing where my father was being held and no one, despite my mother's pleading, would tell her. Visit after visit to City Hall and to the Central Police Station left her in helpless frustration. Nobody knew anything, or if they did know, they didn't tell her. All we did know was that other men from our block had also been taken, like my father, in the night. All sons who were 18 and older were also taken with their fathers. But so far, no women and children. This news was small comfort to us.

I was forbidden from going to school and so was my sister Lotte. We were not permitted to buy food in shops that were owned by Germans. Our winter coats hung in the hallway, with their yellow stars sewn on the front, to identify us as Jews. We stayed in our apartment, quiet and terrified, as if our father was already dead. But it was my mother who was a beehive of activity. She left the house early every day and returned only at dinnertime. Her usual carefully prepared meals dwindled into cold suppers. We ate always in silence. If Ilse asked about our father, my mother would only cry. My good, kind, gentle father, the neighborhood doctor, who gladly and willingly treated every patient with the utmost kindness and consideration—it was unbearable to think we might never see him again.

At long last through the Jewish community group my mother had finally found out where my father had been taken. He was in a concentration camp, Dachau, that had been set up in Germany, one of many, to hold Jews and other undesirables who were thought to be a threat to the purity of the Aryan race.

In these still early years of Hitler's plan, "The Final Solution"—to wipe out every non-Aryan in Germany and the occupied countries—it was still possible, if you had the money, to purchase a prisoner's freedom. That is, IF you had the money. And IF you were prepared to leave Germany immediately afterwards.

My mother—how did she manage it alone? She gathered from our apartment everything of value: silver candlesticks, her gold earrings and bracelets, my father's gold watch—whatever she could turn into cash and took these to a pawnshop. One day she left with a large bagful of Deutschmarks, and when she came home, her bag was empty. In two days, my father, pale and thin, appeared at our door, in the very same clothes he had worn on the evening he was taken.

In those six weeks in the camp, he had become a very old man. We four gathered around him, clutching him to us and wept silent tears of thanks.

We had less than 48 hours to pack and leave the country. My mother and father were now both in a frantic race with the clock. Passports and visas to purchase, tickets to be bought. Our treasured belongings that had been with our family for generations had to be left behind. We could only take what we could carry. And just enough money to cover our expenses. We were not allowed to take any of our family's savings. No money was allowed to leave Germany.

My parents purchased five first-class tickets for passage on the German ship, the *St. Louis*, which was scheduled to depart from Hamburg for Cuba on May 13, 1939. They also purchased "landing certificates" from a Cuban government official for $160 each that would permit us to land, legally, as immigrants, in Cuba. We had a plan!

We traveled from Augsburg to Hamburg by train, always watching behind us, never knowing when a tap on the shoulder would mean my father would be taken away again. When we finally climbed up the gangplank of that beautiful ship, I felt that we would all be able to breathe again. Never in my life had I felt such terror as in the last two days.

At the top of the gangplank, Captain Schroeder stood in his smart blue uniform, with his cap with the gold braid on the visor. He looked at our family of refugees, smiled and said, "Welcome aboard!" I let out a long sigh. Safe at last.

The ship, to my eleven-year-old eyes, was a palace. The food was delicious. I had ice cream for dessert every day. Ice cream! The ship even had a swimming pool on our deck. If the past six weeks had been hell, this now was surely heaven.

Heaven lasted two weeks and then the nightmare returned. When we reached Cuba, the 936 refugees were not permitted to land. The Cuban officials invalidated our landing certificates. After several days of negotiating, 22 of the passengers were permitted to land, leaving the rest of us abandoned to our fate.

Captain Schroeder dropped anchor in Havana harbor not knowing where to turn. When he radioed back to Germany, he received the command: RETURN TO GERMANY AT ONCE. If he did that, Schroeder knew that certain death awaited his passengers. For several days he disobeyed the orders, while radioing desperately to the United States and Canada. Would these governments allow the ship to land the refugees who were fleeing for their lives?

When the Cuban officials insisted that the *St. Louis* leave Havana harbor, Schroeder made one last attempt to reach the Canadian government, telling them that there were only 914 refugees seeking safe haven. Wouldn't the Canadians let them enter? Only 914?

The response from Prime Minister Mackenzie King's government in Canada was short and brutal: Only 914? None is too many.

Study Questions

1. As you see it, what are the significant issues in this case?
2. From the information in the case, what can you tell about what life was like for the Jews in Germany in 1939?
3. What do you suppose it might be like—can you imagine it—to live in a country where government officials are not only allowed, but commanded to come to your home and take a member of your family away, only because he or she was of a certain religion or race or sexual

orientation? What do you suppose made that possible in Germany during the Nazi reign of terror?
4. As far as you know, where does this happen today?
5. How do you suppose so many people come to hold racist beliefs? The beliefs that people of different races or religions are "undesirable?"
6. What kinds of Immigration Laws keep "undesirables" out of countries where they would be safer? What explains the reasons behind these laws?
7. This case is an example of racial hatred in its most extreme form. Can you give examples from your own experiences, in which racial or religious hatred has touched you or someone you know?

Follow-Up Materials

Books

Frank, Anne (1967). *The Diary of Anne Frank*
ten Boom, Corrie (1984). *The Hiding Place*
Thomas, Gordon & Morgan, Max. (1974). *Voyage of the Damned*
Hersey, John. (1988). *The Wall*
Macdonald, Maryann. *Odette's Secrets*

Films

The Number on My Great Grandfather's Arm; *The Book Thief*; *The Courageous Heart of Irene Sendler*; *Run, Boy, Run*; *Island on Bird Street.* (Most adult films about the Holocaust are, in this writer's opinion too realistic and full of horror for middle graders. While these few seem more age appropriate, it is suggested that teachers preview them before including them as follow-up options.)

CASE 3: I STILL HAVE NIGHTMARES!

Notes to the Teacher: Ruby Bridges was six years old when she was "tapped" by the Equal Justice Initiative, in November 1960, to become the first Black student to integrate the all-white William Frantz Elementary School in New Orleans. With the approval and sanction of both parents, Ruby, escorted by four United States deputy marshals, braved the screaming, cursing, taunting crowds that lined up on the streets to protest, and made her way into the school, where she would be attending first grade.

The Supreme Court of the United States had declared segregated schools unconstitutional by passing Brown v. Board of Education in 1954. But six years later, schools were still segregated in the southern states.

When Bridges entered the school, all the other students stayed home. For the rest of the school year, it was only her and her teacher. Crowds continued to appear, shouting curses, taunting, and threatening. "I used to have nightmares," Ruby told interviewers many years later. "I remember being very very frightened." There was retaliation against her family; stores refused to sell to her parents and her father lost his job in the Park Service. But despite all of that, Ruby made it to second grade and by then, the school's incoming first grade class had eight Black students.

The big ideas on which this case is built are:

1. In the American South since the Civil War, Black children were taught in segregated schools, which were badly funded, lacked adequate teaching materials, and were housed in run-down buildings.
2. Black children were expressly excluded from attending all-white schools.
3. In 1954, the United States Supreme Court Chief Justice Earl Warren delivered the unanimous ruling in the landmark civil rights case Brown v. Board of Education of Topeka, Kansas, citing that state-sanctioned segregation of public schools was a violation of the 14th amendment and was therefore unconstitutional.
4. The precedent that "separate-but-equal" education and other services was overturned. "Separate but equal" was not equal at all.
5. Despite the ruling, many southern state schools continued to keep Black children out of all-white schools.
6. The passage of the Civil Rights Act of 1965 began the process of desegregation in earnest.
7. But it took a lot of initiatives by Black citizens in the south to break these racial barriers, at the risk of their lives.

Case: "I Used to Have Nightmares!"

The four men came into the kitchen, with their badges pinned to their jackets and their guns tucked into their belts. Ruby Bridges was just finishing her breakfast while the four men stood, silently, waiting for her. She was dressed in her new red pinafore, with a white blouse and a Peter Pan collar. Her mother had braided her hair and put a pink ribbon at the top. She was ready for her first day in first grade at her new school.

Ruby was only six years old. She didn't understand why she was being transferred to a new school. She was happy in kindergarten in her old school and she had a lot of friends there. But her mother had said, "You are going to a new school. So just be brave and behave."

Her mother put her sweater over her shoulders and Ruby went out the door, with two of the Federal Marshals in front of her and two behind—encasing her in a kind of box. Four very tall men walking ahead and behind a very small, very young Black girl, dressed in her new red pinafore, carrying her book bag at her side.

Along the street from her house and on the way to school the sidewalks were jammed full of very angry grownups, yelling, chanting, cursing. Some of them were throwing things. But the Federal Marshals were careful that nothing hit Ruby and they continued walking. At the entrance to the William Frantz Elementary School in the city of New Orleans, the crowds were huge and the yelling and cursing were louder and more threatening. Ruby didn't understand; but she knew enough to be frightened, very frightened.

In her later years, when she was asked about that first day at school, she said, "I still have nightmares about it. I was terrified."

When Ruby entered her first-grade classroom, she was the only student there. None of the white children were present. They had all stayed home from school. Ruby and her teacher were the only ones in the class—just the two of them in that large classroom. The white children stayed at home for the rest of the school year. And the crowds chanting and yelling and cursing never stopped, but Ruby continued to go to William Franz Elementary School for the rest of the year.

By the next year, a trickle of white students began to come to school and slowly, the school's enrollment became a mixture of Black and white children. And slowly the crowds thinned out and finally dispersed. And the sky didn't fall as Black and white children sat together, played together, and learned together at the William Franz Elementary School in New Orleans, Louisiana.

Study Questions

1. How would you summarize the important events in this case? What do you consider to be the main ideas?
2. How come, in your view, it took more than 100 years after the Civil War, for Blacks to be permitted to ride busses, eat at lunch counters, and go to the same schools as white people in the American south?
3. What, do you suppose, allows people to hold onto their racist beliefs? What hypotheses can you suggest?
4. Ruby Bridges' family were among those who, some at great risk to their personal safety, took the steps that led to further integration of the races in the southern states. What, do you suppose, makes it possible for some people to take those steps?
5. What do you see as some of the long-lasting effects of what Ruby Bridges did in 1960?

6. What, in your opinion, still needs to be done to insure the end of racial discrimination?

Follow-Up Materials

Books

Bridges, Ruby. *Ruby Bridges Goes to School: My True Story*
Coles, Robert. *The Story of Ruby Bridges*
Hood, Susan. *Shaking Things Up*
Jazynka, Kitson. *Rosa Parks*
Jazynka, Kitson. *Martin Luther King*
Kramer, Barbara. *Harriet Tubman*

Films

And the Children Shall Lead; *Hidden Figures*; *Pride*; *Sounder*; *To Kill a Mockingbird*; *Mudbound*; *The Color Purple*; *Conrack*. (N.B. It's always a good idea for teachers to preview the films before showing to the class—just to make sure that the film is age appropriate.)

See, also, the Norman Rockwell illustration of Ruby, escorted by Federal Marshals: http://www.nrm.org/thinglink/text/ProblemLiveWith.html

CASE 4: IT BREAKS MY HEART!

Notes to the Teacher: In November, 2020, President-Elect Joe Biden announced that at the top of his agenda as president would be climate change. This would include two primary goals: to have a carbon-free electricity grid by 2035 and to have a net zero-carbon economy by 2050. "Climate change is cumulative; the longer we wait, the harder it gets to solve. There is rising alarm and evidence of a warming planet; the world has been cooking itself for decades."

For some, such an initiative is the merest beginning of the need to rectify the environmental problems that are increasing the dangers to planet earth. Organizations, businesses, and people that are striving for sustainability is increasing. Green Peace is "passionate about protecting the earth," working to bring about change through political lobbying, citizen action, and consumer pressure. The Green Family's purpose is to help householders reduce the amount of rubbish sent to landfill. Green Choices encourages people to make ecologically sound decisions in living their everyday lives.

Yet, humans are continuing to generate too much trash that cannot be dealt with in a sustainable way. Waste that is not biodegradable and cannot be properly recycled is filling our oceans and landfills. Making our environment cleaner is an uphill battle, for which every person on planet Earth may play a role.

The case, "It Breaks My Heart" looks at one event that illuminates how the ocean has become a dumping ground for human waste and the implications of that on marine life.

The big ideas on which this case rests are:

1. Waste disposal is a huge concern for us and our environment.
2. Pollution threatens ecosystems and endangers many species.
3. Waste that is not biodegradable and cannot be properly recycled is filling our oceans and landfills.
4. Every one of us can play a role in reducing pollution, no matter how small.

Case: It Breaks My Heart!

The young whale was laid out on the table, stretched end to end, its gaunt body a testament to his starved condition. The marine mammal expert began to cut away to see if he could figure out what caused the whale to starve to death in an ocean that was full of food. The whale had wasted away, its skeleton showing through the sagging skin. Dr. Andres Rafel, curator of the marine museum used his sharp knife to cut an opening in the whale's stomach. He couldn't believe his eyes at what he saw.

Dr. Rafel's young son, Danillo, was standing next to his father, watching him perform the autopsy, horrified at what he saw coming out of the whale's body. Plastic and more plastic bursting out of its stomach. One huge bag, another huge bag, and then more than 16 sacks, snack bags, and big tangles of nylon rope. The plastic trash was so tightly packed in the whale's stomach that it felt like a huge hardball. When Dr. Rafel weighed the plastic, there was more than 88 pounds of it. No wonder the whale starved to death. It was unable to consume any real food; the plastic had jammed up his digestive system.

Danillo looked at the poor young marine mammal and tears began to form in his eyes. "How could this happen, dad?" he asked his father. "How could our beautiful ocean have become a dumping ground for plastic waste? It breaks my heart to see this poor whale that starved to death."

Dr. Rafel put his arms around his son to comfort him. He said, "It's a wonder how this poor creature could have lasted this long. He must have suffered terribly."

Danillo left the room, his eyes still wet with tears. He was determined to find out what he could about the plastic in the ocean, to see if he could do something to get the oceans cleaned up. What he found was shocking to him.

First, he learned that this young whale died of starvation and dehydration that was brought about by the plastic stuffing its belly. Its body was unable to digest the plastic waste, and as a result no food could be digested. Danillo also found out that plastic pollution contributes to the death of other species, not only whales, but dolphins, birds, and fish—who are found dead with their stomachs full of plastic too. As Danillo's research grew, he discovered that UNESCO estimates that more than 100,000 marine mammals die each year because of plastic pollution.

Danillo lives in Davao City, in the Philippines. In his reading and research he found that his country was one of the most prolific plastic polluters in the world, and many of its waterways are filled with trash. When he finished reading up on the destruction that was caused by plastic waste being dumped into the ocean he decided that he would go on a one-person crusade to see if he could help to reduce plastic pollution in not only his country but all over the world. He began by creating his own website: Danilloagainstplastictrash.com and asked for volunteers to join his crusade.

"Does anyone have any ideas about how we can begin? About what we can do? Send your messages to me @Danilloagainstplastictrash.com."

Study Questions

1. What do you see as the main issues in this case? How would you summarize them?
2. What, in your view, explains the starvation of the young whale?
3. What do you suppose explains the reasons for people dumping their trash into the ocean?
4. How, in your view, does the dumping of waste products in the ocean impact marine life?
5. What explains the popular need for the use of plastic products? How do plastics improve our lives? What do you see as some negative features of plastic use?
6. What do you suppose we can do to lessen our dependence on plastic? What do you suppose we can do to help restore the purity of the oceans?

Follow-Up Activities

Books

Hiaasen, Carl. *Hoot*
Torday, Piers. *The Last Wild*
Medina, Nico. *Who Was Jacques Cousteau?*
Clinton, Chelsea. *Start Now! You Can Make a Difference*
Allen, Kate. *The Line Tender*
Morpurgo, Michael. *Why the Whales Came*

Films

Wall-E; *Hoot*; *Free Willy*

CASE 5: I KNOW WHAT I LIKE!

Notes to the Teacher: Voting, a basic foundation of a democratic society, is the right and responsibility of each eligible adult. It has been said that the strength of a democracy is dependent, to a large extent, on an informed electorate. The assumption is made that as people exercise their right to vote wisely and thoughtfully, based on knowledge and data, their choices become informed choices.

This case presents a situation in which delegates are assembled to select a candidate for mayor in a municipal election. The case highlights how factors other than competence weigh heavily in people's choices.

The case should open the door to the examination of how alternate criteria such as personality, appearance, slogans, oration style, emotional appeal, misinformation, and other factors result in the election of less than competent candidates.

Big ideas on which this case rests:

1. Voting is the right and responsibility of each eligible adult in a democratic society.
2. Voting occurs at various levels and in various contexts of the electoral process.
3. The strength of a democracy is largely dependent on an informed electorate.
4. How voters make decisions about whom to vote for is dependent on a variety of factors, not all of them "rational."

5. Voters are vulnerable to pressure from different sources, like TV ads, the Internet, Facebook postings, Twitter, op ed articles in newspapers, editorials, news articles, and misinformation.
6. Different groups with their own agendas use different means to win voters' confidence and support.

Case: The Best Breakfast Gets My Vote!

The smell of freshly baked cinnamon buns came wafting down the hotel corridor as Brian and Harriet made their way to the meeting room. "Mmmmm" Brian said. "That's making my mouth water. I haven't had any breakfast yet."

Harriet nodded. "Me too. I hope the coffee is hot and fresh. There's nothing worse than coffee that has been standing around for a day and a half."

The pair opened the door to the meeting room. It was already filling with delegates who were there to choose the mayoral candidate for their party's ticket. This was a once-in-four-years occasion, where delegates from a political party would gather and choose the best person for the job. Many factors were at stake in their choice, and the decision was never easy. There were four candidates who wanted the job.

The voters of this midwestern city had already identified their priorities—those important issues which the newly elected mayor should address if elected. Concern for the environment, waste disposal, the local parks, schools, and recreation facilities were at the top of the list of public concerns. The candidate selected to run on this party's ticket should, at least, be sympathetic to these concerns, as well as having some idea of how he or she was going to implement them if elected to office.

In preparation for this meeting, each candidate had set up a table with refreshments for the delegates' breakfast. One table, sponsored by Earl Watson, had a basket of rolls, jams, and sliced fruits. A second table, put together by the team of Janet Spires, offered freshly baked cinnamon buns, croissant, assorted muffins, and a big basket of oranges. A third table, laid on by Frank Forman, had an urn of coffee, another urn of tea, and a platter of assorted biscuits.

A fourth table had a large espresso machine offering not only espresso but café latte and cappuccino, eggs benedict, rashers of bacon, and sausage kept warm in a large, oval chafing dish, fresh fruit salad, and an assortment of Italian pastries. This was sponsored by Kate Maloney's team.

"Look," cried out Harriet. "Kate Maloney has some eggs benedict. They are my absolute faves. My mouth is watering."

Brian was quick to respond. "I don't know about those eggs. Get a load of what Janet's team has. Enough croissants to feed an army and look at that basket of muffins. Cranberry-orange, pecan, and banana chocolate chip! But I'm stuck on those cinnamon buns. I think I'll just stick around here."

Harriet tugged at his arm. "Listen, you can't let yourself be persuaded by cinnamon buns, no matter how many or how delicious. You've got to decide on the person, not on the breakfast."

"I know. But it's hard, especially when I love cinnamon buns. I think that the person who lays out the best breakfast must be the best person. After all, she must be thinking of how hungry we are and that has to count for something," Brian said.

Harriet watched the delegates move from table to table. The smiling candidates were hovering over their breakfast buffets, hoping that their food might make a difference to their chances. And Harriet thought, "Well, if it depended on the breakfast, it would be Kate Maloney, hands down." It was hard not to be persuaded by the food.

Finally, the delegates sat down, with platters of food in their laps to listen to the speeches of the candidates. Brian's plate had two large cinnamon buns, an almond croissant, and three different kinds of muffins. He was so consumed with the food that he hardly listened to what the candidates were saying. Breakfast and speeches finished, the delegates were ready to cast their votes.

Harriet looked at Brian, picking up the last bits of crumbs from his plate. "I think that Kate made the best speech. I think she is the one who has the best interests of our city at heart. She is getting my vote. Of course, I also thought her breakfast buffet was the best."

Brian looked as if he was ready for a nap. "I don't know. I think they were all good. So why not let the one with the best breakfast get my vote?"

Study Questions

1. What do you see as the important issues in this case? Which do you consider to be the most important?
2. In your view, is it possible for voters to be persuaded by a strategy like providing a dazzling breakfast to those casting a vote? In your experience, what other factors may influence voters in making their choice?
3. From your knowledge and experience, what are some strategies used by candidates to persuade people to vote for them?
4. How can a voter be certain that what is being presented by a candidate is accurate and fair? What ideas do you have about that?
5. In your view, what might be some "good ways" for people to make their choices in an important election?
6. What are your ideas for helping people make better choices in important elections?

Follow-Up Activities

Books

Yacka, Douglas. *What is a Presidential Election?*
Gutman, Dan. *The Kid Who Ran for President*
De Capua, Sarah. *A True Book: Civics: Voting*
Sullivan, George. *Scholastic Book of Presidents*
Benoit, Peter. *Cornerstones of Freedom: Women's Right to Vote*

Films

The Candidate; The Best Man; State of the Union; The Last Hurrah; All the Kings Men; A Face in the Crowd; Wag the Dog; Dave; Napoleon Dynamite; Idiocracy (N.B. These films are more mature—intended for more adult audiences but are highly relevant to the political process. Teachers may find one or more suitable for their older classes.)

CASE 6: HOW COULD THIS HAPPEN IN A DEMOCRACY?

Notes to the Teacher: In the justice system, the rule is that everyone, regardless of social position or power, must obey the law of the land. Nobody is above the law, including those who govern us. Under the rule of law, everyone is equal. Rich or poor, male or female, native born or new citizens are all equal before the law. The rule of law guarantees everyone fundamental justice: the right to a fair and impartial trial.

Independent judges apply the rule of law equally, without prejudice.

The big ideas on which this case rests are:

1. Equality before the law and the right to a fair trial are the cornerstones of the legal system in a democracy.
2. Justice is dispensed by those in the justice system, according to their interpretations of the law.
3. While laws are written to protect citizens and to promote peaceful resolution of conflicts, the interpretation of the law, the dispensing of justice, is the job of those who administer the criminal justice system.
4. Although laws are written and explicit, the ways in which they are interpreted by those in the system allow them freedom to exercise their own judgments and make their own decisions.
5. Interpretations of the law are influenced by these people's ability to make intelligent judgments of the data, free from their personally held biases.

6. In some cases, factors like personal bias, racial bias, gender bias, and the "need to win a case at all costs" influence the way justice is dispensed.

Case: How Could This Happen in a Democracy?

The courtroom hushed as the jurors filed in to take their seats in the jury box, only four short hours after they had begun their discussions. Their faces were set in stone and it was impossible to predict how they had decided. But it did not look good for Donald Marshall Jr.

The court clerk rose and turned to the jurors. "Have you reached a verdict?"
"Yes," said the jury foreman.
"Do you find the accused, Donald Marshall, Jr. guilty or not guilty?"
"Guilty," the foreman replied.

All eyes in the courtroom shifted to Donald, except for his father, who buried his face in his hands. The verdict was too much for him to bear. His 17-year-old son had just been convicted of murder. Even though Donald had sworn he was innocent, swore over and over that he had not killed anyone, that the police had the wrong man, he was going to jail for a long, long time.

In the justice system, there is a guarantee of justice to everyone. All persons are entitled to a fair and impartial trial, no matter the color of their skin or their social class or their ethnicity. Donald had his fair trial. Or did he?

The judge turned to the teenage boy and asked him to stand up. With a solemn face, the judge pronounced the sentence: life imprisonment. Donald hung his head and wept.

Dorchester Penitentiary is a maximum security prison. It sits on top of a hill, looking like a fortress. Stone walls, three feet thick, topped with barbed wire, and armed guards with dogs patrolling the grounds—the toughest prison in the country. Inside the cell blocks, prisoners spend from 10 to 15 hours a day in cells that are 60 square feet each. Five times a day the prison population is counted. Each day passes in grinding monotony.

When the door to his cell closed, Donald remembered his last visit with his parents just before they took him away. His father told him that his lawyer had an appeal going and that maybe he would be out before too long. His father then asked Donald one more time:

"Donald, did you kill Sandy Seale?" And once again, Donald told his father, "No, dad. I didn't do it."

That last visit with his family at the county jail would have to last Donald for a long time. Neither his parents nor his friends had the money to travel from their home to visit him—a distance of hundreds of miles. No visits, no food baskets, nothing from home to soften his life, to make the days pass. Just the hard, stone cell and the daily mind-numbing grind.

At age 17, Donald should have been out in the world enjoying the life of a typical teenager. Instead he was locked away for life, without even a chance of parole, unless he freely admitted his guilt. Wasn't that bizarre? Here he was in jail forever, for a crime he did not do, and he stood no chance of parole unless he admitted he was guilty. Isn't there something wrong with this picture?

Eleven years is a long time to endure the injustice of knowing that you have been convicted of a crime you didn't do. In eleven years, Donald Marshall went to bed 4,000 nights in his prison cell wondering how this nightmare could have happened to him.

Donald Marshall Jr., age 17, was a Micmac Indian. He and buddy Sandy Seale, a 17-year-old Black boy were walking through a park in the center of town. They had both wanted to go to the dance, but the tickets were already sold out. Sandy had to be home at midnight, it was his curfew. It was almost midnight when they were met by Roy Ebsary, age 59, a former ship's cook, and Jimmy MacNeil, 25, an unemployed laborer. Ebsary, who had a police record of other violent crimes, was drunk.

Ebsary took out a knife and said, "This is for you Black man," and he thrust the knife into Sandy's stomach. Then he lunged at Donald, cutting him on the arm. Donald ran for his life. At the edge of the park, he ran into Maynard Chant, age 14, who was on his way home. "Look what they did to me," Donald said, pointing to the cut that was bleeding on his arm.

"Who?" asked Maynard.

"Two fellows over in the park. My buddy's over there with a knife in his stomach."

The two boys flagged down a car to get help and when they got back to Sandy Seale, he was lying in a pool of blood, saying, "I'm gonna die."

By the time the ambulance arrived Sandy had lost too much blood. After the interns stitched up Donald's arm, he walked down the corridor to check on his friend. Donald remembered thinking, "That guy had so much blood all over him, his whole body was shiny." Sandy Seale died at 8 o'clock the next evening. A few days later, two detectives arrested a dumbfounded Donald Marshall Junior for the murder of his friend.

Eleven years is a long time to wait for justice to be done. Donald was a man of 28 years when he was finally released and acquitted by the Court of Appeals. Three years later the government of Nova Scotia appointed a Royal Commission to look into the facts of the case, to determine how one boy could be the victim of a miscarriage of justice, and to get to the bottom of how this could happen.

The findings of the Royal Commission were shocking for anyone who believes in justice. The Commission found the following damaging errors in bringing Donald to justice:

1. The police response was entirely inadequate, incompetent, and unprofessional.
2. The investigation by the lead detective was inadequate, incompetent, and unprofessional.
3. There was no evidence to support Marshall's guilt in the crime.
4. The fact that Marshall was a Micmac Indian was one reason he was identified as a suspect.
5. The detective ignored evidence from witnesses that supported Marshall's story.
6. The prosecutor failed to interview key witnesses that supported Marshall's story.
7. The defense counsel failed to provide adequate professional representation of Marshall.
8. The trial judge made fundamental errors in hearing the case.
9. The police made an incompetent investigation of the case.

The Royal Commission summed up its findings: "The criminal justice system failed Donald Marshall, Junior at virtually every step, from his arrest to his wrongful conviction." They concluded that: the tragedy of the failure of the justice system is made worse by the evidence that this miscarriage of justice could and should have been corrected quickly if those involved in the system had carried out their duties in a competent manner. That they did not do that is due, in part, at least, to the fact that Donald Marshall, Jr. is an Indian."

Study Questions

1. As you see it, what were the events that led to the arrest of Donald Marshall? How would you summarize them?
2. In your view what factors might have led to the prejudice against Marshall in this case?
3. What is your understanding of the way the justice system works to protect and defend the innocent? What is your understanding of the way the system works to convict the guilty?
4. The rule of law is that "everyone is equal before the law." If this is the rule of law, how do you explain what happened to Donald Marshall?
5. What recourse does a citizen have when he or she is wrongfully accused? What is your understanding of how this works?
6. How does prejudice influence thinking? How does a person's biases get in the way of making good decisions? What examples can you give of how this works?

Follow-Up Activities

Books

Lee, Harper. *To Kill A Mockingbird*
Ryga, George. *The Ecstasy of Rita Joe*
Griffin, William Howard. *Black Like Me*
Brown. Dee. *Bury My Heart at Wounded Knee*
Draper, Sharon. *Stella By Starlight*

Films

The Thin Blue Line. A documentary film of how racism prevents equal treatment before the law of Blacks in the United States; *To Kill a Mockingbird*; *Justice Denied*. National Film Board treatment of the true story of the case of Donald Marshall; *Pride*; *Sounder*. (N.B. Once again it's a good idea for teachers to preview these films to make sure they are age appropriate for their classes.)

CASE 7: A CRISIS OF PANDEMIC PROPORTIONS!

Notes to the Teacher: The Spanish flu, as it was nicknamed in 1918, killed more than 50 million people all over the world in less than a year. It was more deadly than World War I, which was raging in Europe and which was responsible for the slaughter of millions of men on the battlefields. The flu spread rapidly; some died quickly. Others who had fewer symptoms, but were nonetheless ill, were disease carriers. It was considered the deadliest virus of the century.

Scientists at that time were not sure where the disease originated, and why it spread so quickly. Despite the very quick spread of the disease, there was no quarantine, no adequate medical supplies, and not enough doctors and nurses to help the seriously ill. Governments in war torn countries were more concerned with fighting the war than with fighting the disease.

What explained the quick spread of the pandemic? The medical officers who were looking out for the men scheduled to embark for the battlefields were not on top of keeping the virus contained. They allowed the men to go abroad, with the already infected ones serving as plague carriers, spreading the infection worldwide. It has been said that World War I was the main reason for the spread of the Spanish flu.

The case serves as a backdrop to open inquiry into how disease spreads, the causes of a pandemic, and some of the steps that can be taken to contain it, with an eye toward the more recent COVID-19 pandemic.

The big ideas on which this case rests are:

1. The Spanish flu, a worldwide pandemic that occurred in 1918–1919 was responsible for the deaths of more than 50 million people worldwide.
2. The origin of the virus was not known at the time. Scientists had fewer resources to treat the disease.
3. Ignorance of how lethal the disease was accounted for its rapid spread. There was no quarantine, no vaccine, no orders for containment. Governments were more concerned with fighting the battles of WWI than they were about the Spanish flu.
4. Soldiers from the United States who were infected were sent across the Atlantic Ocean to fight, which spread the disease worldwide.
5. Knowing the details about the spread of the Spanish flu helps scientists in their fight against COVID-19.

Case: A Crisis of Epidemic Proportions

Jim Harris, a private in the United States Army was feeling sick. He was waiting in a barracks in Boston, along with his fellow soldiers, to board a troop transport that would take them across the Atlantic Ocean to the war zone in Europe. The battlefields in France were a killing zone. Millions of men, Germans and Allied soldiers, had already been slaughtered in the trench warfare that was an unbelievable nightmare. The United States, coming late into the fight, was now armed and ready to send men to replace those lost.

Jim had no doubts that this was a cause worth fighting for. He was ready to give his life for his country. But the sore throat he was feeling was telling him that perhaps he was not ready to go. Maybe he needed to see a doctor?

He looked over at his buddy, Nat Keegan, whose face was already pale and sweaty.

"Hey, Nat," Jim called. "Are you feeling sick too? I've got this very sore throat coming on and I think I should see the doctor."

Nat began to crumple and sat down quickly on his bunk. "Yeh, I'm feeling pretty lousy myself. I don't know if I'm just afraid of what we will be facing over there, or whether I'm really coming down with something."

Jim said, "I know what you mean. But this throat is really sore. It's becoming hard for me to talk. Let's go over to see the medic and see what he says."

The two men picked up their gear and headed for the infirmary. What was a surprise to them was the long line up of men who were already waiting to see the doctor. They took their place in the line and began the long wait. One man dropped to the floor and was lifted up by his buddies and sat on a chair. A second man dropped down as well. This was beginning to look serious.

The doctor looked over the men, one at a time, and pronounced them sick, but not sick enough to keep them from boarding the ship. He gave them some aspirin and told them to make sure to drink a lot of water. Even though some of the men had a high temperature, were coughing, and sweating, and had trouble breathing, the doctor passed them as "fit" to go overseas to fight the enemy.

On board the ship, many of the men got worse. Pvt. Jim Harris was having trouble breathing. He said to his best buddy Ken, "I think I'm dying, Ken." Ken was having trouble breathing himself and was gasping for air. In less than four hours, both men were dead. Ken and Jim, along with 13 other men, were buried at sea, never having reached the European shore.

How was it possible that such fine young men, in the prime of life, healthy and fit, could get sick and die in less than two days? What was going on here?

In the next weeks, more and more soldiers and civilians got sick and died. The doctors that were seeing patients quickly became aware of the obvious. This was not an epidemic; this was a pandemic—an epidemic that occurs in many locations all over the world. It was spread, to a large extent, by the ships that went everywhere, carrying soldiers who were infected. It was spread at home when sick soldiers returned to their families, hugged and kissed them and made them sick as well.

Many years later, as doctors and scientists re-evaluated what happened during the pandemic of the Spanish flu in 1918–1919, they realized what they could have done to prevent the spread of the disease. Even without a vaccine, there should have been regulations to stop travel, to quarantine those who were already ill, to keep people from infecting each other by containment and by wearing masks.

What lessons have been learned from the Spanish flu to help in dealing with the pandemic of 2020?

Study Questions

1. What do you consider to be the important ideas of this case?
2. What in your view, explains the very rapid spread of the Spanish flu?
3. What do you suppose doctors and medical officers might have done to prevent its spread at that time?
4. Sometimes, when faced with a tough decision, like whether to send a sick soldier off to war, or to keep him home and care for his illness, a doctor has to choose what's more important. What was more important in that doctor's choice? In your view, how would you judge that decision?
5. What lessons have we learned from our knowledge of the Spanish flu, and "disease control" that applies to the COVID-19 pandemic? What are your ideas about it?
6. What do you see as each person's responsibility in a time of pandemic?

Follow-Up Activities

Books

Berger, Melvin. *Germs Make Me Sick*
Gardy, Jennifer. *It's Catching. The Infectious World of Germs and Microbes*
Rooke, Thom. *A Germ's Journey*
Senec, Taylyn & Shafiq Uzma. *Keep Away from Germs*
More sophisticated books include:
Barry, John. *The Great Influenza*
Getz, David. *Purple Death*
Editors, Charles Rivers. *The 1918 Spanish Flu Pandemic*
Zinsser, Hans. *Rats, Lice and History*
Barnes, Barry & Arnold, Dee. *Germs are Germs* (case): see: https://www.sfu.ca/education/centres-offices/ec/resources/biology.html

Films

The Spanish Flu—The Forgotten Fallen; *Outbreak: Anatomy of a Plague*; *We Heard the Bells*; *1918*. (N.B. Teachers are reminded that these films may not be appropriate for middle graders. Previewing before showing is highly recommended.)

CASE 8: NOBODY WANTS ME HERE!

Notes to the Teacher: Immigration in America has long been a contentious issue. While at one time America's borders were more open, welcoming refugees seeking asylum, there were also times when severe restrictions were imposed, limiting the chances of those wanting to immigrate (see, for example: The Page Act, 1875; Chinese Exclusion Act, 1882; Immigration Acts, 1891, 1903, 1907, 1917, 1918, 1924, 1952, 1990; Emergency Quota Act, 1921; Homeland Security Act, 2002). More open and more closed borders generally reflected the priorities of those in power and were often a sign of the political ethos of an era.

Immigrants leave their countries for many reasons, including: looking for a better quality of life, looking for safety when home conditions are inhospitable (e.g., war, famine, political duress, racism, economic hardship, limited opportunities), the draw of western civilization (e.g., personal political freedom, material "things").

Despite restrictions on immigration, the data are clear that half the projected growth in the U.S. population comes from new immigrants. "Overall, immigrants are estimated to add about $10 billion a year to the economy" (Bracey, 1999). Studies show that overall, the impact of immigration is positive. A Department of Labor report under the Bush administration called the perception that immigrants take American jobs "the most persistent fallacy about immigration in popular thought" (Arce, 2019).

This case highlights some of the reasons people choose to emigrate and the hardships they face when they try to make new lives in their adopted country.

The big ideas on which this case rests are:

1. Economic conditions in the "receiving" country dictate the conditions that invite or deny admission to immigrants.
2. Immigrants leave their native countries for many reasons, including fear for their safety, the search for more opportunities, and economic hardship at home.
3. Leaving home requires a dislocation, both physical and psychological, from the social/cultural fabric of their home country.
4. Life in a new country means facing many unanticipated hardships, such having to learn a new language, disconnection from one's original culture, racism, and simple logistics, like finding a job, or an affordable apartment.
5. Establishing oneself in a new country requires perseverance, tough mindedness, courage, smarts, flexibility.
6. In the overall, immigrants make substantial contributions to the culture and the cultural fabric of their new countries.

Case: Nobody Wants Me Here!

Ousmane looked at the alarm clock. It was just 5:30, the sky was still dark, and his room was cold. He shivered as he put on his jeans and slipped his feet into his worn-out shoes. He had to walk down the hall to the toilet which he shared with the other tenants in his single room apartment on the Lower East Side of New York City. The toilet smelled bad, but at least it was inside, and not in the backyard. He got back to his room, ran a comb through his hair, put on his toque and warm jacket, a gift from the homeless shelter, and got ready to face the day.

One of the things he missed sorely in his new life in America was his family, his friends, his culture. But his chances of making a decent life in his home country, Senegal, were zero. There was so much wrong there: great corruption, no justice, and very bad schools. His parents were farmers, who just barely managed to grow enough to pay the rent and buy the food they needed to live. But they did manage to scrimp and save enough money to buy him a ticket to come to America, where he might have a chance for a better life.

Ousmane was one of the large number of teenagers, some as young as 14 or 15, who come without their parents, looking for a better life, for more opportunities, for a chance of success. In their home countries, none of that was possible. It would have been better if he could have come to America legally, but there was no chance of that. His only chance was to come as an illegal, pretending he was just on a visit and always hiding from the immigration authorities.

He was afraid all the time.

Ousmane's work day began before dawn at a diner close to where he lived. He worked in the kitchen, washing dishes, scrubbing countertops, sweeping and mopping floors, from 6 in the morning until 3 in the afternoon. On Sundays when the diner was closed, he had a part time job at a factory where he swept floors.

His small salary was just enough to pay his rent and buy food. Not enough to buy any of the "toys" that American boys of his age love so much, like iPods, smartphones, and tablets with so many games to enjoy. English is a hard language for him to learn, but he kept at it, taking two classes a week at a local high school. He had no friends, no one to talk to, no one to confide in. He was so lonely sometimes that his heart ached.

His dream was to become legal, to become accepted in his adopted country, to be able to speak English well enough to make friends, to get a better job, and earn enough money to bring his parents and younger sister over too. But what were his chances of doing that?

As he shuffled down the street in his torn shoes, people first stared and then looked away as if he was truly an undesirable. But all he wanted was a chance to better himself, to make a decent life.

In his letter to his mother and father, he wrote in desperation, "Nobody wants me here. Nobody talks to me. I'm so lonely. Is this a better life than the one I had in Senegal?"

Study Questions

1. What do you consider to be the main issues in this case? How would you summarize them?
2. What do you see as some conditions in his home country that caused Ousmane to immigrate to America? How did he manage to do that?
3. How come, in your view, it is so hard for a boy like Ousmane to become a legal immigrant?
4. How come there is such negative feeling among the general population against accepting immigrants? What is your position on it?
5. What, in your view, are some of the obstacles that Ousmane faces in his new life? How do you suppose a new immigrant manages those obstacles?

6. Based on your own experiences and readings, what are the some of the contributions immigrants have made to America over the years?

Follow-Up Activities

Books

(N.B. There are literally dozens of books for middle graders that deal with issues of immigration. These are only a few.)

Yans-McLaughlin and Lightman, Marjorie. 1997. *Ellis Island and the Peopling of America*

Freedman, Russell. *Immigrant Kids*

Cobblestone magazine has two theme issues on immigrants: Chinese Americans, Greek Americans, Hispanic Americans, Irish Americans, Italian Americans, Japanese Americans, Jewish Americans, and Polish Americans

Hesse, Karen. *Letters from Rifka*

Lasky, Kathryn. *The Night Journey*

Levine, Ellen. *If Your Name Was Changed at Ellis Island*

Levitan, Sonia. *Journey to America*

Whelan, Gloria. *Goodbye Vietnam*

Choy, Wayson. *The Jade Peony*

Tan, Shaun. *The Arrival*

Jimenez, Francisco. *The Circuit*

Films

The Emigrants; *In America*; *Namesake*; *Don't Ask Me Where I'm From*; *Black Girl*; *The Joy Luck Club*; *Paddington*; *America, America*; *The New Land*; *Brooklyn*; *I Remember Mama*; *The Terminal*. (N.B. Since most of these are "adult" films, teachers are advised to preview them before selecting them for their age appropriate groups.)

CASE 9: IS IT FAIR?

Notes to the Teacher: This case examines the disparity of wealth between a select group of teenagers, who are consumed with the importance of material goods and accumulated wealth, and another group of teens who must struggle to buy the few items they need to survive. The case highlights the gap between those few at the top of the income hierarchy and those at the bottom. An important question that this case poses is: what are the implications of such wealth disparity for a healthy society?

The big ideas on which this case rests are:

1. The aggressive acquisition of money, the primary aim to acquire more, has replaced other, more socially conscious goals in young people entering the work force.
2. The drive for more—more money, more consumer goods, more status, has implications for the economy and for the socio-ethical values of the population.
3. The accumulation and concentration of wealth at the top that has occurred over the last 40 years is not a result of nature, but of government policy. Such accumulation increases the disparity between the "haves" and the "have-nots."
4. The "haves" are able to have more because the "have-nots" have less.

Case 9: Is It Fair?

The auditorium was a sea of closely cropped heads perched atop starched white collars, from which hung the familiar blue school tie. From the podium, the headmaster looked out smugly across the rows of graduating seniors, boys in identical blue blazers with the school emblem marking each pocket, and thought, "These boys are destined to shape the future of this country." As he delivered the commencement address, the graduates sat, pretending to listen, while their young minds dwelt on other, more earthly matters.

Harley Robinson didn't have any difficulty in tuning out the headmaster's speech. He had heard enough of that garbage to last him a lifetime. Now he had other, more important things to think about, like, for example, whether his father was going to come through with the new car he wanted for a graduation present. After all, four years at St. Sinclair's Academy with passing grades deserved at least a BMW. He had done his part, kept his bargain with his father by studying just enough to get by. Now it was his father's turn to deliver the goods.

His eyes shifted to where Charles Howard was sitting and wondered if that punk was going to top him again by getting a Porsche. Charles's mother and father seemed always to make sure that Chas had the best of everything. And Chas was such a jerk. "If Chas gets a Porsche, it's going to make my BMW look like garbage," Harley thought.

The headmaster was now droning on about how the St. Sinclair boys were the finest examples of young manhood in the country. Their parents sat proudly, in their designer clothes, lapping up the flattery with the assurance that they deserved every word.

Finally it was over! The boys threw their caps in the air, that marked the end of the graduation ceremony and parents and graduates stormed the exits for the event that every boy had been waiting for. Around the circular driveway of the school sat a shining circle of brand new cars, their gleaming hoods brightly reflecting the light of the afternoon sun. It looked like some kind of automobile derby.

Fathers handed sets of keys into sweaty young hands and boys raced down the line of cars, trying to match key with lock. There was only one Porsche and Charles's key fitted its lock smartly. Charles stepped in, turned the motor over in a loud thrust, and popped open the sun roof, his grin wide and toothy. There were four BMWs and Harley tried his key in two without luck, before the third one, a sleek green beauty, yielded. The Porsche was THE car; the BMW was only second best.

Harley saw that Donald Granger had wound up with a Mazda RX7. Geez, didn't his dad know that a Mazda was garbage? The Grangers, for all their money had no sense of the right stuff. There were certain brands that counted, certain things you had to have if you were going to show that you were important. A Porsche, or a BMW, or a Tesla, for example, but not a Mazda. A Rolex but not a Seiko watch. A Ralph Lauren Polo and not Levi jeans. If you were going to count for anything, you had to have the right stuff.

Four boys and four sets of parents stood on the sidelines watching the scene of 23 boys scrambling around trying to find their four-wheeled gifts. Paul, Kim, Phillip, and George were scholarship students. They did not pay the $30,000 a year tuition fee that the other families did. St. Sinclair had a policy of providing tuition-free scholarships to four deserving boys each year, but they were never a real part of the tuition boys' group and never included in their parties. How could they be?

They were at St. Sinclair's to study and learn. They were the ones who got the best grades. They were smarter than the tuition boys. Their parents worked hard at jobs that didn't pay much and home life was always a scramble to make ends meet. New clothes were hard to come by and they certainly did not have any of the expensive "toys"—up-to-date computers, the most recent models of cell phones and tablets. They rode their bicycles to school instead of being driven by their mothers in the latest model cars and brought their own lunch, instead of eating in the cafeteria.

When Kim, George, Paul, and Phillip talked together about their school experiences, they couldn't help but be troubled by the difference in the lifestyles of the tuition boys and the scholarship boys. They believed that the tuition boys had all the advantages and would probably end up at high-paying jobs in the best companies in the country, while their own chances for success were fewer and harder to come by.

Was that fair?

Study Questions

1. How do you interpret the title of this case, Is it Fair? What does this mean to you?
2. How do you suppose the drive for more money has become so important? What examples can you give of this?
3. What do you suppose contributes to a person's desire for wealth? How do you explain it?
4. What do you see as the downsides of such acquisition?
5. What in your view, explains the reasons for the difference in income between the "haves" and the "have-nots?
6. How does family income and status affect a person's chances for later success? What are your ideas about it?

Follow-Up Activities

Books

Applegate, Katherine. *Crenshaw*
Jacobson, Jennifer. *Paper Things*
Balliett, Blue. *Hold Fast*
Bremen, Melody. *The Boy Who Painted the World*
Bauer, Joan. *Almost Home*
Ogle, Rex. *Free Lunch*
McKenna, James, and Glista, Jeannine. *How To Turn $100 into $1,000,000*
Clements, Andrew. *Lunch Money*
Karlitz, Gail. *Growing Money*
Merrill, Jean. *The Toothpaste Millionaire*

Films

Les Miserables; *Grapes of Wrath*; *Slumdog Millionaire*; *The Color Purple*; *Places in the Heart*

More Adult Flms

Bicycle Thief; *Billionaire Boys Club*

CASE 10: WHY WON'T ANYONE HELP ME?

Notes to the Teacher: The case of Kitty Genovese drew the attention of people all over the United States and abroad for what it said about the refusal of neighbors to come to the aid of a woman being attacked on the street below their windows.

As Kitty Genovese, a 28-year-old woman was walking down the quiet, residential street where she lived, she was attacked and stabbed to death by a burglar who assaulted and robbed her. During the attack, Ms. Genovese called out repeatedly for help; neighbors in the apartment buildings looked out, saw the attack, and none of them phoned the police. Genovese might have been saved if police arrived in time. But without help, she was left to bleed to death on the sidewalk of the lovely tree-lined street where she lived.

Understandably the case raised a furor of concern; why was it that 38 neighbors, from the safety of their own apartments, viewing the attack, failed to summon help for Kitty Genovese? What did that say about community? About the way people cared for each other? About our human responsibilities?

This case focuses on the meaning of community, feelings of belonging, and a shared human connection and what that means for our human relationships. As Jane Austen has written, "Manners is what holds a society together. At bottom, propriety is concern for other people. When that goes out the window, the gates of hell are shortly opened, and ignorance is King."

The big ideas on which this case rests are:

1. "The only thing necessary for the triumph of evil is for good men to do nothing."
2. A community ethos depends on our shared human connection, our personal relatedness.
3. That shared connection is what makes us more human, less lonely, less isolated, less alienated, more accountable.

Case: Why Won't Anyone Help Me!

"Help me! Help me!" she screamed. "I've been stabbed. Please, someone help me." Kitty lay on the sidewalk, her blood seeping out of the wounds in her chest. Her attacker ran off down the block, got into his car and drove off, leaving the badly wounded woman bleeding to death on the sidewalk just outside of her building.

Kitty, despite her wounds, crawled to her apartment door and lay there, now unable to move. She was finally found by one of her neighbors, who screamed for someone to call the police. By the time an ambulance arrived, Kitty Genovese was beyond help. She died on the way to the hospital.

Kew Gardens, in Queens, New York City, was considered a peaceful, safe area to live. Quiet, residential, tree-lined streets; families with young children, working couples, and retired older people lived in the high-rise apartment buildings on both sides of Austin Street. No one felt unsafe in that neighborhood. How could this happen here?

What was also beyond normal was the fact that 38 people, looking out of the windows of their apartments, heard and saw what was happening on the street below. They did nothing to help her. They didn't phone the police. They didn't phone for an ambulance. They didn't want to get involved.

One man was interviewed afterwards by a newspaper reporter. He said he heard noises and when he opened his window, he saw Kitty lying on the ground, still alive and whimpering for help. He shut his window and called a friend to ask him what he should do. His friend said, "Don't get involved."

How was this possible? What would explain why some people, from the safety of their homes, who were witness to such a crime, would not help a neighbor?

Study Questions

1. What do you see as the important issues in this case?
2. What, do you suppose, explains how it was possible that Kitty's neighbors, from the safety of their apartments, chose to ignore her cries for help? What hypotheses can you suggest?
3. What other examples can you cite in which people in a community helped or failed to help each other in times of crisis? What do you see as the consequences of that help? Or lack of help?
4. What does this case tell you about the ways in which a community serves, or fails to serve its members?
5. Why, in your opinion, should people help each other in times of crisis? What do you see as some important reasons for offering that kind of help?

Follow-up activities

(N.B. There are several references to the Kitty Genovese case on the Web. They are, however adult sources.)

Kassin, S. M. "The Killing of Kitty Genovese: What Else Does This Case Tell Us?"

Manning, R., Levine, M. and Collins, A. "The Kitty Genovese Murder and the Social Psychology of Helping."

The book that offers another aspect of people helping others in times of crisis, is of course, *The Diary of a Young Girl*, by Anne Frank.

There are several films related to the Kitty Genovese case but they are not included as they are considered too adult for middle graders.

Chapter 7

What Me? A Case Writer?

"I'm not a writer," he protests. "I'm afraid I don't have the skills to write a case that my students would want to read."

Writing cases may be a new adventure for a teacher, and for some, it may appear to be an impossible task. Lack of experience with writing makes a person feel like a beginner on a ski slope, the blank page on the computer as forbidding as a steep downhill run, riddled with dangerous grades and curves. Yet with a bit of experience, writing like skiing, can be exhilarating, challenging, and very satisfying. Some teachers even grow to love it.

Not every teacher will want to write his or her own cases. Teachers have other more pressing things to do with their time and good teachers hardly find adequate time to do everything they need to do in the first place. There are already lots of good cases available to choose from (see, e.g., https://www.sfu.ca/education/centres-offices/ec/resources/.htm) and writing one's own case may be a bridge too far.

On the other hand, the cases in this book will not touch all the issues that a teacher wants his or her students to study, examine, explore. There may be an issue that is so important, so pressing, and so needing attention, that a teacher will consider writing a case. And once a teacher has found success in his or her work teaching with cases, that may be more than sufficient motivation to tackle the task.

Should that be the case, some suggestions are offered to that intrepid case writer that may help to ease the pathway to successful endeavors.

CHARACTERISTICS OF CASE NARRATIVES

A brief analysis of what constitutes a case will reveal some attributes that are inherent in cases. It begins with the fundamental principle of all good writing: Good writing is good writing is good writing. In her essay, "Reflections of a Casewriter," Hansen (1987) advises, "In writing, especially narrative prose, less is more; pomposity is boring; and incoherence is a complete disaster. Orwell left me hypersensitive to the power of language to bamboozle and benumb as well as enlighten. Strunk and White left me terrified of being fuzzy or dull, and morbidly averse to the passive voice."

Hansen's (1987) advice for case writers holds as well for writers:

- Consider for whom you are writing. Write in a way that will grab your readers and keep hold of their lapels until you're done with them.
- Recognize the thudding passages in your own early drafts and either throw them out or improve them . . . Soliciting a colleague's opinion at this point can make the difference between good, readable writing and alphabet soup.
- Reconsider the material from a reader's point of view . . . assume that the reader is every bit as intelligent, sophisticated, humorous, overcommitted, fatigued, irritable, emotional, and generally human as you are.
- Involve the reader's five senses, rather than simply the intellect, with imagery that stimulates fantasy.
- Use alliteration and assonance.
- Vary the length and syntax of sentences, using first a short one, then a long one, then perhaps a fragment.
- Put the most important details at the beginning or end of paragraphs.
- Check to see if too many paragraphs begin with participial phrases, or the word *he*, or *whatever*.
- Remember that repetition dulls the mind.

Beyond the general rules for writing good narratives, cases have other narrative features that are uniquely theirs.

The opening of the narrative should draw the students immediately into the story. Cases usually begin with an action mode. The idea is to capture the reader's attention right off the bat, so that no student will respond with "Ho hum, just another boring assignment," but instead, "Wow! What is this? I want to know more!"

(Example: *"My God!" he yelled. "We're sinking!" The captain searched the panel of dials frantically, as if he could find the one that had betrayed him, the one that had caused this terrible accident. The alarms throughout the ship reached screaming intensity, as men scrambled to reach the lifeboats. In the background of the turmoil, the calls, "Abandon ship! Abandon ship!" repeated, like staccato drumbeats, marking time in the chaos.*

Captain Tanaka, his face a gray mask, listened to the sounds of his ship breaking up on the iceberg, its jagged knives of ice cutting through the ship's jugular, spilling its cargo of oil and men into the icy seas. The disaster was incomprehensible. How did it happen? How could this fine, modern supertanker, with its cargo of 500,000 tonnes of crude oil, its state of the art equipment and technology—how could this ship have been defeated by an iceberg?) (Wassermann & O'Shea, *The Case of the Yahagi Maru*, 1992. See https://www.sfu.ca/education/centres-offices/ec/resources/.html for a copy of the case.)

- Cases are built around events of consequence. Issues of substance provide the framework around which cases are written. For example, a case about planting a garden won't go far, but a case about urban dwellers who were fighting for the right to use a vacant lot to plant a neighborhood garden would likely provoke greater attraction and curiosity.
- Cases often elevate tension between two conflicting points of view. Because cases involve the examination of complex issues, there are often several sides to the issue. Good cases elevate these tensions, so that readers are stimulated to discuss them. For example, in the case "How Can I Make A Difference" (Wassermann, 1993) a teacher wrestles with his values about teaching in an inner-city school vs. his friend's encouragement to "pack in the slum school and head for the suburbs where life for teachers is so much sweeter." A good case is never an editorial for one particular point of view; never a polemic for the "right way to think."
- Cases are written so that readers grow to care. The main players in a case are sympathetic characters, and even as they are drawn in complexity, we care about them, about their predicament, about the events that are occurring around them. For students to care, characters must be more than stereotypes. They should be multifaceted and be presented with human failings.
- Case narratives must be believable. In some ways, cases are more akin to good journalistic writing than to fiction. If the most important attribute of a case is its ability to stimulate discussion about the issues, the narrative should be closer to fact than fiction. This characteristic allows readers to be drawn into the case. Students are able to project themselves into the situation. "This could happen to me!" Such identification gives a case increased relevance.
- Cases end on the horns of a dilemma. At the end of a case, issues are not resolved. In fact, the opposite is true. The dilemma, or "hook" is left dangling. This, perhaps, more than any other characteristic, is uniquely associated with case writing. This unfinished business gives cases considerable power and may explain why good cases, even years after they have been read and discussed, continue to plague the mind.

These characteristics of cases are not holy writ. Case writers will inevitably find their own style, their own voice, their own way into the process. That is one of the most attractive aspects about case writing—the process allows much flexibility, so many degrees of freedom in which to be creative. Another is that one does not have to aspire to be a Hemingway or to win the Pulitzer Prize for case writers. Students are, by and large, much taken with the cases they study in class. Perhaps it is because even an "average" case is so much more interesting than the material in the textbook.

One develops skill as a case writer by writing cases and using them, reflecting on how they work. Nothing is lost if a case "falls flat." In fact, much is gained and learned. That is what the editing process is all about.

SITTING DOWN TO WRITE

What's the Big Idea?

At the heart of each case, whether in bioethics, mathematics, social studies, or any discipline, is the "big idea"—that central issue that the case will open to examination. For example, cases in mathematics may use probability theory to make predictions, plotting coordinates in locating objects, error, and uncertainty in measurement, using statistics to manipulate data. Cases in social studies may examine issues such as the relationship between immigration and the economy, the role of lobbyists in influencing legislation, the media as a force in shaping voter choice, the constitutional right to bear arms vs. gun control legislation.

These are only the smallest number of examples of what "big ideas" look like. The range of big ideas underlying any course of study is vast. They point in the direction of what we want students to study, to know, to understand about the course content.

The first task then is choosing from the array of "big ideas" in the curriculum, those that seem more significant, that would lend themselves readily to thoughtful, intensive examination through a case narrative. Obviously, considerable class time will be spent in examining what is chosen, so the big idea should be one of substance, one that is worth that kind of time investment.

WHAT IS THE STORY?

At its best, a case is a darn good story. As you try to imagine your case, think about the story you will tell.

If the big idea concerns immigration, perhaps there is a story about a family of Salvadorian refugees who were illegal aliens and were made to return to their country. Perhaps there is a story about a Mexican family trying to cross the border into Arizona. Perhaps the story is about a woman who lost her job because her employer could get illegal immigrant help for less cost.

Newspapers and magazines are good sources of ideas for case narratives. There are often articles that bear on issues related to a particular social studies issue. Textbooks are also good sources for case narratives. For example, while a science text deals with the depletion of ocean fish stocks as a factual event, one case writer used the data from the text to build a story about the dilemma facing a family whose income was dependent on salmon fishing.

Personal stories may also be woven into case narratives. Teacher-case-writers bring to their writing a vast array of personal experiences which find their way into the stories. These personal events add real-life qualities to cases because they have come from real-life experiences. There are many stories in the Naked City and case writers will find ways imaginative and wonderful to incorporate them into case narratives.

WHO ARE THE CHARACTERS?

Above all, the characters in a case must give the appearance of being real. This is accomplished by "breathing life" into them. People are complex; they do funny things. Sometimes they are irrational. Sometimes they are unpredictable. People have certain attributes. They may prefer Hawaiian pizza to pizza with pepperoni. They may like certain cartoons. They may prefer certain kinds of movies. They may be shy, angry, anxious, scared. Breathing life into a character means giving that character a persona and developing him or her into a three-dimensional being.

WHAT'S THE DILEMMA?

A good case builds up to a climax in which the central character confronts his or her dilemma. Often the dilemma hangs on moral or ethical issues. Sometimes a decision has to be made when some important data are unavailable. Sometimes, personal needs get in the way of a character's behaving as he or she thinks they should, ways that make them feel guilty or ashamed.

In facing issues of complexity, characters in cases wrestle with variables that confound them and make them wish for easy answers. These are the "hooks"—the unfinished business on which cases "end."

It is the dilemma of the case that drives the discussion. When the dilemma is real and is perceived by the students to be real; when students are able to project themselves into a similar situation, that will add great power to a case.

If the dilemma is contrived, phony, or false, the case will lose power to draw students into meaningful dialogue.

The dilemma in a case must allow students freedom of choice and must provide for open examination of alternatives in making that choice.

DRAFT, REDRAFT, REDRAFT

This is perhaps the most irritating part of writing for the novice case writer. The bad news is that there is no fast and easy way to write a first rate case narrative. Cases do not fall without effort, from the mind onto the blank page. They are crafted, like clay is sculpted, until the finished product is as close to perfect as it can be made. Sometimes this takes many drafts. Until a writer can accept the "draft, redraft, redraft" as part of the normal process of writing, and until a writer can give up any illusions about producing a final copy in a first draft, the writing process is more likely to be a road of frustration, unrealistic expectations, and disappointment.

The bottom line is that a writer must learn to love that process, as well as the product. A writer has to see the process as satisfying as the end result; has to be willing to enter into that process ungrudgingly. A writer has to be ruthless abut discarding false opening paragraphs and passages that don't ring true; has to be able to scrap an entire first draft and start again from scratch. Writers who are in love with every word they write are doomed. Parsimony is the key to elegance; overwriting as bad as flatulence. Less, as Hansen (1987) reminded us is more.

STUDYING OTHER CASES

One good way to learn to compose a chorale in the Bach style, the music teacher told her student, is to listen to a great many Bach chorales, and analyze how he has constructed them. One good way to learn to write cases is to read many good cases and to analyze how they are constructed. Sometimes reading cases creates a "mind set" for case writing. Good cases will, at the very least, serve as examples and as a departure point for writing.

WRITING STUDY QUESTIONS

Once the case has been written, the case writer shifts gears to the kinds of questions that will be appended to the case—those questions that will serve to heighten the examination of the important issues to be discussed.

Study questions, like cases, have unique characteristics. They are framed in a way that encourages thoughtful examination. They also have a particular "tone." They invite rather than demand. They are clear and unambiguous in what they ask. They are neither too abstract nor too general. They do not lead to a particular answer or point of view. They avoid forced choices.

Some important considerations in writing good study questions include:

- Sequence the questions so that they move from a general summary of the case to case particulars.
- Sequence the questions so that they proceed from observations, to analysis, to challenging.
- Key the questions into the big ideas of the case. The questions should reflect what warrants thoughtful examination.
- The way questions are worded can constrain or promote further student thinking. See the section in chapter 5 that provides information about the kinds of questions used in debriefing a case. These are helpful models for designing study questions.
- Study the questions attached to the cases in chapter 6 and use them as models to design the study questions for your own case.

END NOTES

The teacher who is new to case writing will find that the best way to determine the effectiveness of a case narrative and a list of study questions is to test its effectiveness in the "marketplace." Teaching a case and letting students work over the study questions will give more than enough evidence of its success in the students' examination of the important social issues.

There is nothing lost if a case is not completely effective in its first trial. In fact, much is gained from studying what went wrong, where the weak areas are, and what needs to be done to improve it on its second or third draft.

And as a final note, inviting students to tell what they think about the case and about the questions may give a teacher more than he or she wanted to know! But in the end, that kind of information coming from those who are the primary beneficiaries of the process will be a gold mine of information that should inform teachers as case writers.[1]

NOTE

1. Adapted by permission of the Publisher. From Selma Wassermann, *An Introduction to Case Method Teaching: A Guide to the Galaxy*. New York: Teachers College Press. Copyright © 1994 by Teachers College, Columbia University. All rights reserved.

Chapter 8

Evaluating Students in a Case Method Classroom

It will be obvious from even a cursory glance, that teaching with cases does not lend itself easily to the more traditional methods of evaluation. Short answer quizzes that emphasize specific pieces of information would be discrepant with what students are learning with case studies. Yet, one of the teacher's mandates is to assess student learning. So how might that work in a classroom where students study cases, engage in small group and large group discussions? What are some effective alternatives for teachers using cases?

SOME ALTERNATIVE EVALUATION METHODS

The alternative methods of evaluation that are being suggested in this chapter have been developed and used successfully in many classrooms where teachers have added case method teaching to their traditional teaching methods (Adam, et al., 1991). It would not be an exaggeration to claim that teachers using them have discovered that not only are they successful replacements for more traditional methods, but they are more enthusiastically embraced by students.

Teachers who have been using these case studies will, of course, be using other teaching strategies in their work in other subjects as well. Given that, it does not mean that traditional forms of evaluation will all disappear. It merely means that alternative methods would replace traditional strategies for their work with cases. While giving up marking and grading students' papers may represent a big shift, the payoffs in terms of seeing how students "perform" on these alternatives may more than convince even the most hard-wired believers in written tests.

There are more than a few benefits to using alternative methods of evaluation. For example:

- They can reasonably provide teachers with information about how well students understand complex concepts.
- They provide students with more choice and give them more control over assessment options.
- They allow students more opportunity to reveal their strengths.
- They provide teachers with diagnostic information about students' strengths and areas of needed competence.
- They emphasize self-evaluation as an important means of promoting students' increased awareness, as well contributing to their independence as learners.[1]

The suggestions below are qualitative assessments, and therefore, do not have unequivocally "correct" and "incorrect" answers that can be marked right or wrong. If they are to be "marked" they require teachers to exercise their professional judgment about the quality of a student's work. This should not be difficult, since it is a given that such judgments are a large part of a teacher's repertoire.

As a culminating experience to their work with a particular case, students may demonstrate their understandings of the big ideas by completing one of the following types of assignments. These can be done individually or in teams of two or three.

1. Projects
   - Photograph essays. Collecting photographs that are captioned and demonstrate one or more of the big ideas on which the case is built.
   - Videos
   - Art work
   - Computer projects
   - Interviews—gathering information from personal accounts, oral histories
   - Creating a literary account of a specific event, for example: a book, journal, diary, biography
   - Plays, puppet shows, other dramatic presentations
2. Student presentations
   - Debates
   - Dramatic readings
   - Three dimensional exhibits
3. Field work: The alternatives listed in this category would necessarily require approved preplanning, implementation, and reporting
   - Community service
   - Volunteer work
   - Surveys

- Field trips
- Community study
- Walkabouts
4. Written presentations
    - Research reports
    - Scrapbooks
    - Letters to the editor
    - Diaries
    - Bibliographies
    - Critiques

Of course, these are not the only kinds of culminating activities that students might engage in to demonstrate their growing understanding of the issues involved in case studies. Teachers who are marvelously inventive will likely come up with their own ideas. Students, as well, can be called on to make their own suggestions. But whatever choice is made, such alternative methods give students a wide range of opportunities to demonstrate their understandings of the big ideas of their case studies.

SELF-EVALUATION

The idea of students evaluating themselves is far from new or radical. In fact, self-evaluation has been used successfully for many years, even in the primary grades (MacDonald, 1982). The group of social studies teachers using cases at Centennial Secondary School developed their own self-assessment profile that yielded considerable information about the ways in which students perceived themselves in relationship to the Ministry of Education requirements for the Graduation Program (Adam, et al., 1991).

Using self-evaluation tools does not mean a teacher gives up his and her obligation to assess students. It is rather a means for teachers to gather even more data from students' perceptions of their work. Even more important, it gives students additional agency in determining, for themselves, how they have performed in a particular area of study. This is no small benefit, since students who gain skill and authority in self assessments benefit considerably in their growing independence and self-knowledge.

One example of such a self-assessment instrument for a particular work on a case is offered here:

Name _____ **Date** _____

This self-evaluation report provides you with a chance to think about your work on this case and to make some judgments about how well you fulfilled the requirements.

Use this rating scale in your response:

1. If you believe the statement is true to a great extent, give yourself a rating of 1.
2. If you believe the statement is almost true, give yourself a rating of 2.
3. If you believe the statement is not very true, give yourself a rating of 3.

Preparation

1. I studied the case carefully so that I was able to understand the big ideas.
2. I made some notes about the case so I would be able to refer to them for the study group.
3. The way I studied the case helped prepare me for the small group discussion.

Small group work

1. I was an active participant in the study groups.
2. I had good ideas to share.
3. I listened respectfully to the ideas of the other members of the group.
4. I didn't interrupt when someone else was talking.
5. The ideas I shared helped others to see new and important issues in the case.
6. I was a helpful group member.

Whole class discussion

1. I had good ideas to offer in the whole class discussion.
2. My reading of the case and my work in the study groups helped me to clarify my ideas for the whole class discussion.
3. I felt okay about volunteering my ideas.
4. I listened respectfully to the ideas of the others.

5. The whole group discussion helped me to understand more about the big ideas in the case.

Follow up

  1. I did some additional reading about the case.
  2. I talked about the issues in the case to others after class.
  3. I have grown in my understanding of the big ideas of the case.
  4. I appreciate how using cases helps me to understand more about important social issues.

General

  1. I made fair and accurate judgments to the statements in this self-evaluation.
  2. I see self-evaluation as a way of helping me to see my work efforts more clearly.
  3. What I learned from making my self-assessment will help me in my future work with cases.

Add any other comments you want to make about your work.

END NOTES

A teacher who has committed to use these cases as a means for middle grade students to study and examine some important social issues will, doubtless, look to some alternative means of making assessments of their work. This chapter has offered several alternative routes to making those assessments, along with a sample self-evaluative tool. These are "suggestions"—a sampling of what teachers may use, or depart from, in finding their own ways to assess students' learning.

Experiences with teachers who have used case method teaching and alternative evaluation methods are more than encouraging. One needs only to try, to take a chance, to see what works, to modify and expand, in order to find the best ways of making determinations of the how and the what of student learning. If experience has any validity the prediction is that once on this road, teachers will not easily look back.

NOTE

1. Adapted by permission of the Publisher. From Selma Wassermann, *Introduction to Case Method Teaching: A Guide to the Galaxy*. New York: Teachers College Press. Copyright © 1994 by Teachers College, Columbia University. All rights reserved.

Chapter 9

And Finally . . .

This book has been written during a time of one of the greatest upheavals in the history of the world. A virus, equal to, and perhaps more virulent than the Spanish Flu of 1919 has decimated populations across the globe. The Unites States, to date, is leading the world in numbers of cases and deaths. A vaccine has finally become available, but distribution with respect to whom and how is still a major problem. Despite hard evidence, many people are in denial about the virus, claiming it is a hoax and refusing to take even the most simple precautions about keeping safe and spreading the disease to others.

A presidential election, in which a winner has been clearly established, has been challenged by a sitting president who refuses to concede his loss. The economy has gone into a deep slump due to the fact that the virus has forced the shutting down of business, shops, entertainment facilities, restaurants, and other services, leaving thousands unemployed. A form of protest called "Black Lives Matter" is giving voice to the urgent need to recognize people of all colors as equally important. The conditions of climate change, and the need to protect the environment from further despoliation is more urgent than ever.

None of these issues escapes children in the middle grades. Middle graders are not immune from hearing and seeing what is going on all around them and around the world. In other words, social issues are not only current, but they are immediate, and in many cases, frightening.

To be able to understand the complexities gives us more tools with which to deal with what is happening, with the unknowns. And that is the hope and the purpose of this text—to provide middle graders with the tools to help them understand, to reason, to apply intelligent habits of thinking to discern, to know more, to abandon fallacious and specious reasoning, to widen their perspectives, to embrace what is sound and logical.

Will teaching with cases do all of that? Is it a cry in the wilderness? Of course, teaching with cases is not the only pedagogy to enable children's thinking, to prepare them more adequately for what is happening in the world, and for what is in their future. But given the data so far, teaching with cases goes a long way to achieve just those goals. In fact, effectively carried out, case method teaching may be one strategy that teachers can embrace with some assurance that the cited goals will, in fact, deliver on their promise.

To those intrepid teachers that are using this text and who are making their first attempts at teaching with cases, may the successes you find encourage and enable you to continue to light students' pathways to a better, more thoughtful, more intelligent, more responsible journey into adulthood.

Appendix: Who Makes the News?

Who Makes the News?
Paul Odermatt

Notes to the Teacher This case is concerned with the ways in which events are manipulated by the media, elevating the conflict between straight and biased reporting. The case centers on questions of media responsibility, the dividing line between news reporting and entertainment, and what, of what is seen on television "news," can be believed as "true."

The **big idea** on which this case rests is:

Media reports do not always reflect the true nature or extent of the news they purport to "cover."   *(over)*

(continued)

Important concepts that flow from this idea include the following:

a. A variety of influences in broadcast media cause the raw reality of life to be altered to fit the requirements of "good" television.

b. People often withhold parts of their lives when being interviewed by the media because they want to be perceived in a certain (more favorable) way.

c. People being interviewed by the media often make decisions about what to reveal and what to conceal about themselves.

d. Media reporters have personal biases which make them selective about what they hope to see and hear.

Who Makes the News?
Paul Odermatt

"I'M GOING TO BE ON TV! They want me to be on the news!" shrieked Lori as she bounded into the house. "Mom, I met this TV reporter at school who wants to film me... Mom?"

The silence of the house didn't dampen Lori's excitement. "It's O.K. I just have to clean up my room, 'cause the TV crew and Jenny, my friend from school, will be here in a half hour... Mom? Mom?"

Lori connected with the silence. She was alone and in charge. She fought the slight flush that warmed her face. Her room! It had to be just right!

Details, only details had to be adjusted. She grabbed Sampson, the lumbering stuffed dog who guarded her bed, and flung him into her sister's room. The stack of *Seventeen's* under her night table were turned spine to the wall, and a *Cosmo* placed on top. Pictures of her boyfriend and another one of her family wedged in the frame of her mirror were tucked into the bottom of a dresser drawer. The closet needed the least work. Her favorite outfits were already hanging in the center. She just pushed the others back so more color would show of the ones she wanted to be seen.

The sound of a car door slamming catapulted her downstairs and into an easy chair. Through the curtains she could see that Martin, the TV reporter, Bill, the camera man, and Jenny, had all arrived together.

Earlier in the day, Martin had asked to come to Lori's home to make a videotape of Lori and Jenny putting on makeup and "getting ready" as if they were going to school in the morning. Shooting at 3:30 in the afternoon was the best time for Martin and Bill, because they couldn't start early enough in the morning, and besides, Martin also wanted to talk with them about "teen stuff."

Lori opened the door to a procession of people, microphones, wires, and maybe her chance to be seen by 200,000 people. A wider staircase would have made the trek easier, but eventually everything was plugged in and tested. They were ready.

The makeup session started slowly. At first, Lori felt awkward because she had never been on TV before, and wasn't quite sure what to do. Martin's directions seemed quite straightforward. "Act natural. Do what you normally do and say what you normally say," summed up his words and attitude. Yet, conversation still did not feel right. Lori was afraid she would talk about someone she knew or say something on TV that would embarrass them or her.

With intense concentration, Lori stared at her image in the mirror as she pushed her lip with the lipstick, carefully spreading the color where she wanted it. "There! I'm ready," she smiled, tossing in the words partially for herself and partially for Bill's camera and microphone that hovered over her shoulder.

"Super!" said Martin. "That's going to look just great. Now let's do it again, with both of you together this time."

Jenny giggled as she pulled up her chair between Lori and Bill.

"Lori, would you wipe off what we just did so we can start fresh from the beginning?" asked Martin, holding out a Kleenex to her. "And this time, hold up all the lipsticks in your hand, shuffle through them, and then pick out the one you want. Then start."

Appendix: Who Makes the News?

Lori, puzzled at the collection in her hand, some hers, some Jenny's and others from the discards in her drawer brought out for this occasion. "I've never owned this many lipsticks at one time before," she mused silently to herself.

The afternoon droned on with takes and retakes. As the girls became more comfortable with the camera, their sense of confidence reappeared. "I'm beginning to feel like Tammy Faye! How much more makeup do I have to put on?" giggled Jenny.

"You're doing just great," said Martin, "but we want to make sure that we get it just right."

Putting on perfume was the funniest for the girls. Bill's camera missed the first splash of perfume, so he asked them to do it again. It took three more splashes till Bill and Martin were satisfied. The room just reeked, but Lori realized that no one watching would ever know how badly. The viewers would only see one splash of perfume on their TV sets.

On the third close-up retake of putting on eye shadow and mascara, Lori just couldn't concentrate. She could only feel the tension and pain in her neck from holding her head the way Bill asked. She worried. From eighteen inches away, the giant cyclops camera's eye stared at her, recording every blink, every misplaced eyelash, every stroke of mascara, every blemish the makeup would not hide. "What do they want from me?" Lori said silently. She stopped, took a long breath that almost came out as a sigh, and looked toward Martin.

"Let's take a break," said Martin, as if he read her mind. "We're pretty well done with makeup. We can wrap this here."

As Bill gathered his camera equipment to go downstairs, Martin reminded the girls: "Wear the exact same clothes, makeup, earrings, and shoes tomorrow morning. Every last detail has to be the same so it will look like you are going to class after putting on your makeup."

Eager to cooperate, Lori and Jenny made careful note of what they had to duplicate the next morning.

"Just want to talk abut teen stuff before we go," started Martin. "You know, sex, alcohol, drugs . . ."

Lori looked at Jenny, who was carefully staring into an empty corner of the room. Lori's mind raced, thinking about her answer to the not-yet-asked questions. Martin had promised not to put them on the spot with very personal questions, but he did say that he wanted to know what they thought, and what teens were like.

"How much money do you spend on clothes and makeup in a month?" Martin began.

"Two hundred dollars," chirped Lori, happy with the question, "for clothes, hair, makeup, everything. I have a part-time job and I love to shop."

Jenny's look reminded Lori that she barely made that much at her job. A bit of exaggeration would be hardly noticed, thought Lori.

"What kinds of things do you talk about with your friends?" asked Martin.

"Parties, clothes, dates, fashion, work, school, you know," said Lori, carefully picking her words so she wouldn't make herself, her friends, or the school look bad. She still wanted to have her friends after they had seen her on TV

Silence was her response to Martin's question about what percentage of teens she would say were sexually active. Lori knew about her friends, but she had also heard some far-out stories about some kids and their parties. She thought they were true, but wasn't sure. What if Martin asked more? "I don't know," was what she felt like saying, yet she worried that those words might make her sound like an outsider.

When Martin asked her what kind of drugs were available through her friends or on the underground drug market, Lori felt on the spot. She didn't believe in drug use, and didn't do drugs, even casually. "Marijuana, cocaine and heroin," she tossed the words out. She didn't know if it was true. At least she said something.

Lori longed for the fun of an hour ago, putting on makeup and perfume over and over. If it wasn't right, Martin would ask them to do it again. With the questions now, she wasn't offered a second chance. Talking with her friends about clothes, friends and parties was easy and fun. Talking to a reporter with a TV camera was not.

In contrast to Martin and Bill's arrival, Lori thought their departure couldn't come soon enough. "I hope they use only the parts I'm happy with," she said to Jenny after the TV crew had left. Uncertainty crept in. What would the tape actually show? And would it be real? ■

Study Questions

1. In your view, what parts of the picture presented about teens would be most accurate? What data support your view of what is accurate?

2. In your view, what parts of the picture presented about teens would be least accurate? What data support your view?

3. In this case, certain factors influenced Lori's and Jenny's behavior. How do you explain it? How is a person's behavior influenced by certain conditions in the immediate situation?

4. As you see it, what role did Martin and Bill play in "shaping" the afternoon session?

5. The videotape that was being filmed in this case was scheduled to be shown during "ratings week." How, in your opinion, might this have contributed to the "shaping" of this show?

6. What do you see, when you see a "newscast" on TV? What do you actually know when you view an event on TV? What are your thoughts on what you will see?

Supplementary Resource Materials

BOOKS AND ARTICLES

Greer, Sandy (1990). "The Distorted Mirror," in *Canada and the World*. October, pp. 14–17.
    A look at objectivity in the news media based on the idea that human beings with human opinions write and present the facts we consume as "news."

Gans, Herbert J. (1979). *Deciding What's News*. New York: Pantheon Books.
    Based on several months spent in television and magazine newsrooms, Gans looks at *CBS Evening News, NBC Nightly News, Newsweek,* and *Time,* to see how the news media portray America and why they portray it the way they do.

FILMS

Double Vision (NFB, 28 min.) Why is the same event often reported differently in the English and French language media? In an attempt to answer this question, the film makers went to the press gallery at the Quebec National Assembly and interviewed English and French speaking journalists. They discuss the reasons for the discrepancy between English and French language news coverage.

The World Is Watching (NFB, 59 min.) This film investigates how American TV news is reported from Nicaragua. The film reveals how the TV network decision-makers change the focus and facts from what the field reporters in Nicaragua actually gathered in order to fit American concerns.

Only the News that Fits (NFB, 30 min.) A half-hour video version of *The World is Watching*.

History on the Run: The Media and the '79 Election (NFB, 57 min.) This documentary film examines a three-week segment of the media's coverage of the federal election of May, 1979. It looks at journalists in action and gives an opportunity to glimpse political figures behind the scenes and their attempts to manipulate the media.

All the President's Men (1979, 138 min.) A feature film starring Dustin Hoffman and Robert Redford that tells the story of two reporters who found a few shreds of evidence and then followed their hunches to uncover the Watergate story.

Broadcast News (1987, 131 min.). Feature film offering a human look at the growing link between news and entertainment in a world where news content is increasingly influenced by the profit motive. With William Hurt, Albert Brooks and Holly Hunter.

Source: Paul Odermatt

Bibliography

Adam, Maureen. 1991. "Teaching with Cases in Grade 11 Social Studies: An Examination of Outcomes Related to the Ministry of Education Graduation Program Goals." Unpublished Master's Thesis, Faculty of Education. Burnaby, BC: Simon Fraser University.

Adam, Maureen, Chambers, Rich, Fukui, Steve, Gluska, Joe, and Wassermann, Selma. 1991. *Evaluation Materials for the Graduation Program.* Victoria, BC Ministry of Education.

Arce, Julissa. 2019. "Trump's Anti-Immigration Rhetoric Was Never About Legality. It Was About Our Brown Skin." *Time*, August 6, 2019.

Bickerton, Laura, Chambers, Rich, Fukui, Steve, Gluska, Joe, McNeill, Brenda, Odermatt, Paul, and Wassermann, Selma. 1991. *Cases for Teaching in the Secondary School.* Coquitlam, BC: CaseWorks.

Bracey, Gerald. 1999. "The Impact of Immigration." *Phi Delta Kappan*, January, 1999, p. 407.

California State Board of Education. 2017. *United States History and Geography: Making A New Nation.* Sacramento: California Department of Education.

Carkhuff, Robert R. & Berenson, David H. 1983. *The Skilled Teacher.* Amherst, MA: Human Resources Development Press.

Christensen, C. Roland and Hansen, Abby. 1987. *Teaching and the Case Method.* Boston: Harvard Business School.

Christensen, C. Roland, Garvin, David, & Sweet, Ann. 1991. *Education for Judgment: The Artistry of Discussion Leadership.* Boston: Harvard Business School Press.

Coles, Robert. 1990. *The Call of Stories.* Boston: Mariner Books.

Dewey, John. 1938. *Experience in Education.* University of Illinois: Kappa Delta Pi.

Ewing, David. 1990. *Inside the Harvard Business School.* New York: Times Books.

Gragg, Charles. 1940. "Because Wisdom Can't Be Told," in the *Harvard Alumni Bulletin.* Boston: Harvard Business School.

Hansen, Abby. 1987. "Reflections of a Casewriter: Writing Teaching Cases." In C. Roland Christensen & Abby Hansen. *Teaching and the Case Method*. Boston: Harvard Business School Press.

Hood, Eileen. 1992. *The Hockey Card*. Simon Fraser University; Case Clearing House. http://www.sfu.ca/education/centres-offices/ec/resources/.html.

Kleinfeld, Judith. 1989. *Teaching Cases in Cross Cultural Education*. Cross Cultural Education Studies. Fairbanks, Alaska, Center for Cross Cultural Studies.

Lawrence, Paul. 1953. "The Preparation of Case Material," in *The Case Method of Teaching Human Relations and Administration*. Ed. Kenneth R. Andrews. Cambridge, MA: Harvard University Press.

MacDonald, Cheryl. 1982. "A Better Way of Reporting." *B. C. Teacher*, Vol. 61, pp. 142–144.

McNeill, Brenda. 1991. "A Conflict of Cultures," in Bickerton, et al. 1991. *Cases for Teaching in the Secondary School*. Coquitlam, BC: CaseWorks.

Odermatt, Paul. 1991. "Who Makes the News?" in Bickerton, Laura, Chambers, Richard, Dart, George, Fukui, Steve, Gluska, Joe, McNeill, Brenda, Odermatt, Paul and Wassermann, Selma. *Cases for Teaching in the Secondary School*. Coquitlam, BC: CaseWorks.

Rutenberg, Jim. 2020. "The Attack on Voting." *The New York Times*, September 30, 2020.

Shulman, Judith. 1992. *Case Methods in Teacher Education*. New York: Teachers College Press.

Silverman, Rita and Welty, William M. 1992. *Case Studies for Teacher Problem Solving*. New York: McGraw Hill.

Wassermann, Selma. 1991. "The Case of Swallowed Pride," in Bickerton, et al. *Cases for Teaching in the Secondary School*. Coquitlam, BC: CaseWorks.

Wassermann, Selma. 1993. *Getting Down to Cases*. New York: Teachers College Press.

Wassermann, Selma. 1994. *Introduction to Case Method Teaching: A Guide to the Galaxy*. New York: Teachers College Press.

Wassermann, Selma. 1992. "A Case for Social Studies." *Phi Delta Kappan*, V. 15, No. 10, pp. 793–801.

Wassermann, Selma. 1990. *Serious Players in the Primary Classroom*. New York: Teachers College Press.

Wassermann, Selma. 2009. *Teaching for Thinking Today. Theory, Strategies and Activities for the K-8 Classroom*. New York: Teachers College Press.

Wheatley, Jack. 1986. "The Use of Case Studies in the Science Classroom." *Journal of College Science Teaching*, 15, 428–432.

Index

Augsburg, Germany, 49, 51
Austen, Jane, 75

behavioral standards, 10
bias, personal, xviii, 7, 61, 62, 65
Biden, Joe, 55
big ideas, 46, 53, 56, 58–59, 61–62, 66; in case writing, 82; identification of, 3, 45; instructional design teaching of, 20; interactive process questions analysis of, 34; Is It Fair? case on, 72; Nobody Wants Me Here case in, 69; None is Too Many case and, 48; Who Makes the News? case in, 96; Why Won't Anyone Help Me? case and, 76
"Black Lives Matter," 93
Bridges, Ruby, 52–55
Brown v. Board of Education, 52–53

The Call of Stories (Cole), 20
case method teaching: additional resources use in, 4; "A Case of Injustice in Our Time" class as, xi; classroom scene in, 1–2; debriefing and small group and whole class discussion in, 1–2, 4; homework assignment in, 1, 4; Hood and elementary school use of, xvi; implications of, 15–17; media events manipulation case in, 1, 96–102; middle grade level students and, x–xi; no judgment in, 3; pedagogy association of, x; schools of education attention to, x; "sticks to your ribs" quality in, ix–x, xii; student comments and reactions on, xi, 3, 5; student interest stimulation and learning goals in, 3–5; teacher beliefs and, xi–xii, 8; teacher questions about, xv; teachers enthusiasm and role in, x, 4; teaching career before, ix; traditional approach opposed to, 4; vitality and critical thinking promotion in, 5–6
case method teaching, middle grades, x–xi, xvii; case writing courses for, xvi; roots of, xv; secondary schools use of, xv; social issues and, 93–94; social studies teachers and, xvi; student comments on, 3, 5; textbooks on, xvi
case method teaching, social issues and, 32, 45; ambiguities wrestling in, xvii; "Black Lives Matter" as, 93; complexities and understanding in, xvii, 93; contemporary situations in, xviii; curriculum guides role in,

xviii–xix; economy slump as, 93; election fraud as, xviii; emotional component in, xix; issue selection in, xviii–xix; middle grade curriculum and, xvi–xvii; middle graders and, 93–94; pandemic as, xviii, 93; pedagogy and teachers regarding, 93–94; personal bias in, xviii
case method teaching, teachers and, x, xv–xvi, 4, 79, 93–94; behavioral standards in, 10; control relinquishing in, 7–8; curriculum covering for, 9–10; debriefing skill and self-scrutiny in, 8; grades and engagement in, 9; learner's independence promotion in, 8; noise and, 10, 16; parent notification in, 10–11; responsibility abandonment feeling in, 8; student control and teacher facilitation in, 7; student grading criteria for, 9; teacher compatibility with, 11; teacher needs and beliefs in, xi–xii, 8; teachers' workshop scene in, 7
"A Case of Injustice in Our Time," xi
cases: "big ideas" identification in, 3, 45; "Case of Swallowed Pride" in, 40–43; as complex educational instruments, 3; "A Conflict of Cultures" as, 31–34; A Crisis of Pandemic and Epidemic Proportions as, 65–68; follow-up activities for, 45; How Could This Happen in a Democracy? as, 61–65; I Know What I Like as, 58–61; I Read it on The Internet as, 45–47; Is It Fair? as, 72–75; I Still Have Nightmares as, 52–55; It Breaks My Heart as, 54–58; Lawrence on, 4; narrative form of, 3; Nobody Wants Me Here as, 68–72; None is Too Many as, 47–52; small group study questions for, 45; social issues in, 45; Who Makes the News? as, 96–102; Why Won't Anyone Help Me? as, 75–77

case teachers, preparation for: case study and questions familiarity in, 14; choice and consequences in, 15; classroom student debate scene in, 13; debriefing skills acquisition for, 13–14; follow-up activities for, 13–14; higher-order questions use in, 16–17; interactive dialogue awareness for, 14; negative idea re-evaluation in, 16; nonsequential learning comfort in, 16; projects use in, 17; student active engagement in, 13; student learning control and evaluation in, 16; student responsibility and, 15–16; student surveys and, 16; students debriefing comments, 14–15; teaching framework understanding in, 13–14; upside and downside of, 17
case writing, xvi; big idea central issue in, 82; capture reader's attention in, 80–81; case effectiveness in, 85; curriculum choosing in, 82; dilemma confronting and discussion in, 83–84; draft and redraft process in, 84; events of consequence in, 81; experience lack in, 79; flexibility and freedom and believability in, 81–82; fundamental principle of, 79; Hansen advice on, 79–80; "hook" dangling in, 81; idea sources and personal experiences for, 83; story imagining in, 82–83; study questions writing and considerations for, 84–85; sympathetic and multifaceted characters for, 81, 83; teachers and, 79; two conflicting points of view in, 81
Centennial School Case Study Project Team, 17
Centennial Secondary School, British Columbia, x, 89
Chambers, Rich, xi
Chant, Maynard, 63
Civil Rights Act, 53

"cold calling," 34
Cole, Robert, 20
"A Conflict of Cultures" case, 31–34
control, 7–8, 16
COVID-19 pandemic, xviii, 40, 43, 45, 66, 68, 93
A Crisis of Pandemic and Epidemic Proportions case: big ideas in, 66; doctors and scientists re-evaluation of, 67; follow-up activities for, 68; quick disease spreading in, 65–66; soldier disease spreading and death in, 67; soldiers illnesses in, 66–67; Spanish flu and World War I in, 65, 66; study questions for, 68
curriculum, xvi–xix, 9–10, 82

Dachau concentration camp, 50
Davao City, Philippines, 57
debriefing process: active listening in, 23; art and craft of, 23–24, 43; Ewing on, 22–23; examine and re-examine skills in, 8, 24; interactive process and, 32–33; no right answers in, 23; stage setting in, 23; student roles in, 23; teacher preparation for, 13–15; as "teaching a case," 22; whole class discussion in, 1–2, 4
Dewey, John, xvi
dilemma confronting, 83–84
discussion, 1–2, 4, 31, 34–35, 83–84
Disney, Walt, Jr., 46
Dorchester Penitentiary, 62
draft and redraft process, 84

Ebsary, Roy, 63
engagement, xvi, 9, 13
Equal Justice Initiative, 52
evaluation, case method classroom students, 16, 22; alternative methods and benefits in, 87–88, 91; data gathering in, 89; field work and projects and student presentations in, 88–89; payoffs in, 87; qualitative assessments for, 88–89; self-assessment report for, 90–91; self-evaluation in, 89; student learning assessment and, 87; student work perceptions in, 89; written presentations in, 89
Ewing, David, 22–23

field work, 88–89
"Final Solution," 48, 50
follow-up activities, 52, 55, 58, 71–72, 74–75, 77; cases and, 45; case teacher prep for, 13–14; A Crisis of Pandemic and Epidemic Proportions case with, 68; How Could This Happen in a Democracy? case with, 65; I Know What I Like case and, 61; instructional design and, 27–28; interactive process and, 40–43; I Read it on The Internet case and, 47

Genovese, Kitty, 75–77
Great Depression, 40–43
Green Choices, 55
Green Peace, 55

Hansen, Abby, 79–80
Harvard Business School, x, xv
higher cognitive level thinking, x, 39
Hitler, Adolf, 49, 50
Hood, Eileen, xvi
"hook" dangling, 81
How Could This Happen in a Democracy? case: big ideas in, 61–62; Dorchester Penitentiary description in, 62; fair and impartial trial entitlement in, 62; follow-up activities for, 65; injustice in, 63; last parental visit in, 62–63; Marshall, Jr., jurors in, 62; Micmac Indian and, 63–64; murder conviction and life imprisonment sentence in, 62; Royal Commission investigation and findings in, 63–64; rule of law in,

61; story of, 63; study questions for, 64–65; teacher prep for, 19–20, 29n1

I Know What I Like case: big ideas in, 58–59; candidate competency in, 58; candidate refreshment for delegates in, 59–60; follow-up activities for, 61; food persuasion use in, 60; informed voting choices in, 58; issues concern in, 59; mayoral candidate choosing in, 59; study questions for, 60

immigration, 48, 68–69

injustice, xi, 63

instructional design, case method teaching: appropriate interventions in, 22; big ideas teaching in, 20; Cole on stories in, 20; debriefing process in, 22–24; emotional and cognitive "weight" in, 20; follow-up activities for, 27–28; group difficulty and, 22; idea airing and articulation and practice sessions in, 20–21; Marshall, Jr., case teacher prep in, 19; need to know in, 27; "post hoc" evaluation in, 22; reflection climate creation for, 24–27; safe climate in, 21; small group work in, 20–22; story enchantment and, 20; student own choices and results in, 28; supplementary material for, 27; teacher neutrality in, 22; teacher-student interactions modeling in, 21; time allocation and "unfinished business" in, 28; topic or issue selection in, 19–20

interactive dialogue, 14, 27

interactive process, tools of: analysis of ideas responses for, 38–39; basic response "play back" and caveat for, 36–37; big idea questions analysis in, 34; case debriefing in, 32–33; case review preparations for, 32; "Case of Swallowed Pride" debriefing and follow-up activities in, 40–43; challenging questions caveats in, 39–40; "cold calling" in, 34; "A Conflict of Cultures" case in, 31–34; debriefing art in, 43; dialogue and, 14, 27; discussion skills for, 34–35; facts highlighting in, 32; higher cognitive level questions for, 39; listen, attend, and apprehend conditions in, 35–36; question choosing and framing for, 38; reflective responses use in, 34; respond invitations in, 38; response categories and selection in, 35, 36; response mirroring for, 37; social issues formulating for, 32; student response safety in, 37; teacher discussion guidelines in, 31; teacher response judgment in, 36; "why" questions and, 39

I Read it on The Internet case: big ideas of, 45–46; disinformation topic in, 45; follow-up activities for, 47; friends and Disney e-mail in, 46–47; new cell phone in, 46; scam accusation in, 47; study questions for, 47; Twitter sign on and, 46

Is It Fair? case: big ideas in, 72; follow-up activities for, 74–75; new car graduation competition in, 73; proud parents in, 73; senior graduation in, 72–73; study questions for, 74; tuition boys and scholarship boys difference in, 73–74; wealth disparity theme in, 72

issue selection, xviii–xix, 19–20

I Still Have Nightmares case: big ideas in, 53; Bridges and white school integration in, 52–54; *Brown v. Board of Education* relevance in, 52–53; crowd reaction and deputy marshals escort in, 52, 53–54; family retaliation in, 53; following school year in, 54; follow-up materials for, 55; racial discrimination theme in, 52; study questions for, 54–55

It Breaks My Heart case: Biden primary goals in, 55; big ideas in, 56; environmental problems in, 55; follow-up activities for, 58; Green Peace and Green Choices in, 55; humans and trash in, 56; plastic in ocean research in, 57; plastic trash in, 56; study questions for, 57; UNESCO facts in, 57; website creation in, 57; young whale starvation in, 56

King, Mackenzie, 51

Lawrence, Paul, 4
listening, 14, 23, 35–36

MacNeil, Jimmy, 63
Marshall, Donald, Jr., 19–20, 29n1, 62–65
media event manipulation, 96–102
Micmac Indian, 63–64

neutrality, 22, 25
Nobody Wants Me Here case: adopted country acceptance in, 70; big ideas in, 69; desperation in, 71; English language classes in, 70; family and friends absence in, 70; fear in, 70; follow-up activities for, 71–72; immigrants reasons for leaving home country and, 69; immigration issue in, 68–69; morning routine and work day in, 70; positive immigration impact in, 69; study questions for, 71
noise, 10, 16
None is Too Many case: anti-Jewish sentiment in, 48–49; Augsburg respectability in, 49; Augsburg to Hamburg train trip in, 51; big ideas in, 48; Captain Schroeder rescue in, 48, 51; Dachau concentration camp and, 50; father removal and return in, 49, 50; "Final Solution" victims in, 48; follow-up material for, 52; German ship and Cuban "landing certificates" in, 48, 50; immigration laws and, 48; leaving country and, 50; life and death difference in, 48; no permission to land in, 51; prisoner's freedom purchase in, 50; racial prejudice theme in, 47–48; SS and Hitler in, 49; study questions for, 51–52; yellow stars identification in, 50
nonsequential learning, 16

Odermatt, Paul, 1–2

parent notification, 10–11
pedagogy, ix–x, xv–xvii, 7–8, 93–94
plastic trash, 56–57

qualitative assessments, 88–89

racial discrimination, 47–49, 52, 64–65
reflection climate creation: consistent respect in, 26; evaluative responses and, 25–26; interactive dialogue partnership in, 27; inviting not commanding in, 24–25; neutrality in, 25; response "reading" in, 26–27; "tone" in, 24
"Reflections of a Casewriter" (Hansen), 79
reflective responses, 34
response mirroring, 37
response "reading," 26–27
Royal Commission, Nova Scotia, 63–64

Schroeder, Gustav, 48, 51
Seale, Sandy, 62–63
self-assessment report, 90–91
Simon Fraser University, xvi
small group discussion, 1, 4, 20–22, 45
Spanish flu, 65, 66, 93
"sticks to your ribs" quality, ix–x, xii
stories, 20, 63, 82–83
students: active engagement of, xvi, 9, 13; case method teaching and, x–xi,

3–5, 7, 9; classroom debate scene of, 13; debriefing and, 14–15, 23; higher cognitive level thinking of, x; instructional design and, 21, 28; Is It Fair? case and, 73–74; I Still Have Nightmares case and, 53–54; learning control and evaluation of, 16; response safety of, 37; responsibility of, 15–16. *See also* evaluation, case method classroom students

study questions, 51–52, 54–55, 60, 68, 74, 76–77; case writing and considerations for, 84–85; How Could This Happen in a Democracy? case and, 64–65; I Read it on The Internet case in, 47; It Breaks My Heart case and, 57; Nobody Wants Me Here case in, 71; small group and, 45; teacher prep and familiarity with, 14; Who Makes the News? case in, 101

supplementary material, 27, 102
Supreme Court, U.S., 52
surveys, 16, 88

teachers, x, xv–xvi, 4, 53–54, 93–94; case writing and, 79; How Could This Happen in a Democracy? case prep of, 19–20, 29n1; instructional design and, 21–22; interactive process of, 31, 36. *See also* case method teaching, teachers and; case teachers, preparation for

teaching: good, ix; pedagogy choosing in, ix–x; "sticks to your ribs" and, ix–x, xii; student higher cognitive levels thinking in, x. *See also* case method teaching

time allocation, 28
Trump, Donald, xviii
Twitter, 46

United Nations Educational, Scientific and Cultural Organization (UNESCO), 57

Warren, Earl, 53
wealth disparity, 72
Who Makes the News? case: being on TV in, 98; big idea in, 96; important concepts in, 97; makeup session and direction in, 98–99; media event manipulation theme in, 96; reporter and camera man arrival in, 98; room clean-up for, 98; sex and drugs and alcohol talk in, 99–100; study questions for, 101; supplementary resource materials for, 102; takes and retakes in, 99; uncertainty in, 100

"why" questions, 39
Why Won't Anyone Help Me? case: big ideas in, 76; community meaning in, 75; concern raising in, 75; follow-up activities for, 77; Genovese case as basis for, 75; human connection in, 75; neighbors noninvolvement in, 76; newspaper reporter interview and, 76; study questions for, 76–77

William Frantz Elementary School, New Orleans, 52, 54
World War I, 65, 66

young whale starvation, 56

About the Author

Selma Wassermann is a Professor Emerita in the Faculty of Education at Simon Fraser University. She is the recipient of the University Award for Teaching Excellence. Her 19 previous books include *Mastering the Art of Teaching* (2021), *Opening Minds* (2021), *Evaluation without Tears* (2020), *What's the Right Thing to Do* (2019), *Teaching for Thinking Today* (2009), and *Case Method Teaching: A Guide to the Galaxy* (1994).

www.ingramcontent.com/pod-product-compliance
Lightning Source LLC
Chambersburg PA
CBHW030144240426
43672CB00005B/267